J.F. Ingram

The Land of Gold, Diamonds and Ivory

Being a Comprehensive Handbook and Guide to the Colonies

J.F. Ingram

The Land of Gold, Diamonds and Ivory
Being a Comprehensive Handbook and Guide to the Colonies

ISBN/EAN: 9783337249281

Printed in Europe, USA, Canada, Australia, Japan

Cover: Foto ©Andreas Hilbeck / pixelio.de

More available books at **www.hansebooks.com**

THE LAND OF GOLD, DIAMONDS & IVORY.

THE
LAND OF GOLD,
DIAMONDS & IVORY;

BEING A

COMPREHENSIVE HANDBOOK AND GUIDE

TO THE

COLONIES, STATES & REPUBLICS

OF

SOUTH AND EAST AFRICA.

BY

J. F. INGRAM, F.R.G.S.,

Author of "AFRICAN LEGENDS AND LYRICS."

LONDON:

W. B. WHITTINGHAM & CO., 91, GRACECHURCH STREET.

1889.

All Rights reserved. Entered at Stationers' Hall

W. B. WHITTINGHAM & CO.,
PRINTERS,
91, GRACECHURCH STREET, E.C.
AND
"THE CHARTERHOUSE PRESS,"
44 & 45, CHARTERHOUSE SQUARE,
LONDON.

PREFACE.

THE purpose of this Volume is to present, at one view, a clear, concise and reliable record of the past history and present condition of South and South-East Africa.

A residence of twenty-three years in the regions treated of, together with a long and intimate acquaintance with the native tribes and their languages, has placed the writer in a position to deal practically with the subject.

The letters from the late Herr CARL MAUCH and THOMAS BAINES, Esq., F.R.G.S., which are inserted in the divisions proper to gold and gold exploration, were published, during their lives, in the columns of the *Natal Mercury*, and will be read with especial interest now that their predictions and labours have borne such ample fruit.

The sections devoted to travel and exploration have been compiled from the author's own experiences, while the historical and statistical facts and figures have been collected only from the best and most trustworthy sources. In dealing with political subjects, an effort has been made to avoid vexed questions, and in every way to strengthen the bonds of amity now existing between all classes of the community, both at home and in South Africa.

With respect to the divisions of the country, geographical, rather than historical, sequence has been followed: the intention being to describe the region from south to north.

It is hoped that the work, limited though it may be, will be of service not only to the intending settler, tourist and sportsman, but also to a large and constantly increasing class of readers who, while staying at home, yet regard with sympathetic interest the struggles, the advances, and the successes of a NEW EMPIRE.

Many of the Illustrations are from Photographs taken by the Author. The others are produced from Photographs of South Africa by Mr. ROBERT HARRIS, of Port Elizabeth.

CHAPTER XXIV (page 189) IS SPECIALLY RECOMMENDED TO THE ATTENTION OF THE READER.

CONTENTS OF CHAPTERS.

CHAPTER I.

A SHORT ACCOUNT OF THE DISCOVERY AND COLONISATION OF THE CAPE COLONY, BY THE PORTUGUESE, DUTCH, AND ENGLISH.

PAGE.

Romantic Delusions.—A new Empire.—Will Africa ever become a useful producing country?—The Answer.—Early Explorations.—Artistic Maps.—The reality of Exploration.—Sebastian's Toils.—Inexperience the source of Trouble.—Diaz and De Gama.—Neglect of Africa.—The Dutch Trading Company.—Treaties with the Hottentots.—Van Riebeek's Administration.—Extension of Territory.—Simon van der Stell.—The first Emigrants.—For Conscience Sake.—The African Pilgrim Fathers.—Wise and Liberal Treatment.—Monopoly of Trade.—The first Cloud.—The Beginning of the Dispersion.—Displacement of the Natives.—Checked by the North-East Tribes.—Organisation.—War between Holland and England.—Poverty and Revolt amongst the Settlers.—Appearance of the English Fleet.—The Importance of the Cape as a Naval Station.—William Prince of Orange writes a Letter to the Cape Settlers.—Battle between the Dutch Colonists and English Forces.—End of the Dutch Company.—English Rule Established.—General Craig's Proclamation of Free Trade.—Introduction of Specie.—Disorder in the Colony.—Measure for better Government.—Earl of Caledon and Sir John Cradock.—Fresh Blood Needed.—Introduction of the first English Emigrants.—Settlement of new Arrivals.—Exodus of Discontented Dutch Boers, or Farmers.—Prosperity of the latest Settlers 1

CHAPTER II.

The Cape Colony of To-day.

PAGE.

Area.—Boundaries.—Population.—Table Mountain.—Cape Town.—Population of Cape Town.—Society.—Divisions, Districts and Towns.— Home-like Appearance. — Harbours. — Table Bay.—Simon's Bay.—Mossel Bay.—Algoa Bay.—Port Elizabeth.—Population. — Institutions. — Port Alfred. — East London and Buffalo River.—Railway System of Cape Colony.—Mileage.—Fares. — Produce. — Statistics. — Ostriches. — Manufactures. — Responsible Government.—Religious and Educational Statistics. —Scenery of Cape Colony 13

CHAPTER III.

Physical Geography, Geology and Minerals of Cape Colony.

Mountains and Altitudes.—Plateaux.—Geology.—Gold.—Cango Caves. —Copper.—Coal 27

CHAPTER IV.

Griqualand West and the Diamond Fields.

History of Griqualand West.—O'Reilly's Discovery.—Annexation of the District.—Star of South Africa.—Establishment of Diamond Mines.—Kimberley and other Mines.—Features of Diamondiferous Deposits.—Weather.—Confidence Established.—Yields of Individual Mines 30

CHAPTER V.

Pondoland and the Pondos.—St. John's River, &c.

Arcadian Beauty.—The Gates of St. John's River.—The Place of Echoes.—Mountain and Flood.—Climate.—An infant Colony.—Territorial Divisions. — Extent. — Griqualand East. — Pioneer British Settlements.—Tembuland.—Transkei.—The Pondomese. —Acquisition of St. John's River Territory.—Arrival in Exploring Steamer.—The Settlement.—Glorious Scenery.—Afloat on the

River.—Jeffery and his Fatal Hunt.—Sharks.—A Moonlight Scene.—Baboons.—The Mineral River.—Leopards and Reptiles. —White's Settlement.—Weaver Birds.—An Interview with the King of Pondoland.—Rivers of Gin.—Estimates of Population.— Sport 34

CHAPTER VI.

SKETCH OF THE EARLY HISTORY OF NATAL.

A Christmas Gift.—Portuguese Explorations.—Shipwrecked Mariners. —Slave Traders.—Physical Alterations.—Early Descriptions.— Chaka's Invasion.—Fire and Death.—Arrival of the English.— Protecting the Natives.—Petty Jealousies.—Advent of the Emigrant Boers.—Their Adventurous March Overland.—Battles and Disasters.—Retief and his Party.—The Promised Land.— Mission to Dingaan.—Treachery and Murder.—War.—Death of Dingaan.—Victory of the Boers.—Republic of Natalia.—Anglo-Dutch War.—The Colony Established 46

CHAPTER VII.

NATAL OF TO-DAY.

Area.—Boundaries.—View from the Sea.—The Harbour and Bay.— Durban.—Population.—Pietermaritzburg.—Situation.—Population.—Towns and Villages.—Railways.—Fares.—Government.— Defence.—Physical Geography and Production.—Total Population.—Locations.—Distribution of Land.—Rules and Regulations for Disposal of Land.—Additional Productions.—Imports and Exports.—The Geology of Natal and South Africa.—Gold and Minerals... 53

CHAPTER VIII.

THE UMZIMKULU RIVER.—PORT SHEPSTONE AND OTHER PORTS.

The King's Execution Place.—Description of Harbour and Lagoon.— Up Stream.—St. Helen's Rock and Rapids.—Marble.—The Vengeance of the Bees.—Umkomas.—Scotburg.—Umzinto.— Produce 76

CONTENTS.

CHAPTER IX.

ORANGE RIVER FREE STATE AND BASUTOLAND.

PAGE.

Boundaries.—Population.—History of the Free State.—Griquas.—Emigrant Boers.—Sir Peregrine Maitland's idea.—Sir Harry Smith.—War.—Proclamation of British Authority.—Abandonment.—War and Rumours of War.—Sir J. Brand.—Peace and Prosperity.—Language.—Geography.—Divisions.—Education.—Basutoland.—Boundaries.—Moshesh.—Missionaries.—Annexation and Divisions.—Population.—Government.—The Tribes of Basutoland.—Wealth.—Grain and Cattle.—A Future Field for Royal Academicians 79

CHAPTER X.

BRITISH BECHUANALAND.

Boundaries.—Chiefs.—Protectorate.—The Natives.—Moselekatzie, the Lion of the North.—The Bechuanas.—Climate.—Rev. Mr. Mackenzie's Views on Emigration 84

CHAPTER XI.

THE TRANSVAAL REPUBLIC.

Moselekatzie.—Griquas.—Defeat of Matabele and retreat to present country.—Influx of Boers.—Andres Pretoria.—Establishment of the Transvaal Republic.—Effect of Diamond Fields and Lydenburg Gold Fields on the Transvaal.—Burgers.—Annexation to England.—Restoration.—Riches untold.—Geography 87

CHAPTER XII.

EARLY ACCOUNTS OF GOLD IN AFRICA.—MONOMOTAPA.

Traces of the Dead.—The Ophir of Scripture.—Josephus and East Africa.—Dos Santos on Ancient African Geography and History.—Carl Ritter.—The Queen of Sheba.—Herr Carl Mauch.—Dr. Petermann's Summary of his Work.—Rev. A. Merensky.—Letters from Mauch.—Description of Ancient Ruins 90

CHAPTER XIII.

BAINES AND HIS LABOURS.—HUNTING ADVENTURES IN MATABELELAND.

PAGE.

Thomas Baines.—Matabeleland Exploration.—M'Nombati Concessions.—A Buffalo Hunt.—Sketching a Live Lioness.—Rhinoceros Adventure.—In Mashonaland.—Hartley Hills.—Harnessing 150 Warriors.—Feeding a Multitude on Coffee.—Election of Matabele King.—Lo Bengula.—Shooting Wolves.—A Pretender to Deity.—Superstitions.—Theology.—A Buffalo Hunt.—The Sketch-book Bearer.—More Quartz and Ruins.—Latitude.—House building.—Disaster and Death.—Explorations.—The Mashonas.—An Elephant Hunt.—Native Gold Diggers.—Herds of Elephants.—Missionaries and their Labours.—Marauding Parties.—Portuguese interference 105

CHAPTER XIV.

GOLD FIELDS OF TO-DAY.

Trade Depression in the South African Colonies.—The Gold Fever.—A Rush.—Barberton and Moodie's.—Extensions.—Description of De Kaap 129

CHAPTER XV.

THE WITWATERSRANDT FIELDS AND JOHANNESBURG.

Situation.—Early History.—Population.—Rival Routes.—An account of my last Visit and what befel me.—Boers at home.—Progress on the Fields.—Industry.—Johannesburg.—Banket Deposits.—Estimates.—Figures and Measurements.—Purity of the Stone ... 132

CHAPTER XVI.

THE KOMATIE AND OTHER FIELDS.

Steynsdorp.—A Visit to the Natal Fields.—Grand Scenery.—Natives.—"U'shillin."—Zululand Workings 142

CONTENTS.

CHAPTER XVII.

The Zulus and Zululand.

A Tribute of Respect.—Boundaries.—Annexation.—Early History.—The present state of the Zulus.—New Republic.—Apportionment of the Country ... 145

CHAPTER XVIII.

Customs and Legends of Zululand.

Necessity for Travellers, Settlers and Hunters knowing the Superstitions of the Natives.—Reserve of the African Tribes on Sacred subjects.—The Legend of Creation.—Witchcraft, U'Swellaboi and "Evil Ones."—Prophets and Seers.—Marriage Customs.—Children.—Men's Work.—How to treat the African Natives.—Dress.—Food ... 151

CHAPTER XIX.

Swazieland and the Swazies.

Importance of the Country.—Situation.—Trade Route.—Measurements.—Physical Geography.—Game.—History.—The People.—Government.—My recent Exploration, Travels and Adventures in the Country.—Getting an Expedition together.—My Boer friend.—Passage of the Pongolo.—Toils.—Blisterschlapen's Misadventure.—A New No-Man's-Land.—Doctoring Boers.—Fillibusters.—A Peep at Fillibustering Home Life.—A Patriot.—Assagai River.—Inkompeece River.—A joyful Meeting and a Friend in need ... 157

CHAPTER XX.

M'Kaiyan Mountain.—A Peep into the Heart of the "Loneland."—A Panorama worthy of the Land.—The Descent from Temperate to Tropic in Two Hours.—Amongst the Palms.—Gold, Silver, and Copper indications.—Sandhlana, the Prime Minister.—Prince Umkopolo.—An interview with King Umbandine.—Boer methods of acquiring Land.—The King's Appeal ... 164

CHAPTER XXI.

THE HUNTING GROUNDS OF SWAZIELAND.

Monain Kraal.—The Valley of Quartz.—The Trail of Witchcraft and Blood.—Face to face with the large Game.—Wolves.—Off on Foot.—The Cave.—Snakes, Wolves, Vampires, Lions.—At close quarters with the King of Beasts.—Back to the waggon.—Thirst.—A Conflagration.—A Hunt.—Slave dealers.—Partridges.—Danger from Fillibusters.—Gold 170

CHAPTER XXII.

A PEEP AT EAST AFRICA.—DELAGOA BAY.—LORENZO MARQUES.—RAILWAYS.—AMATONGALAND.

Situation.—Geology.—Foliage.—Lorenzo Marques.—Recent Progress.—Geographical Description.—Awaking of the Portuguese.—South African Telegraph Company.—A Field for the Botanist, Naturalist and Sportsman.—Accommodation for Shipping.—Natives.—History of Railway Enterprise.—Opening of Line.—Amatongaland Boundaries.—Government.—Features.—Native tastes.—Directions to Travellers.—Importance of retaining our hold on the Land 175

CHAPTER XXIII.

GENERAL INFORMATION.

Routes to Gold Fields.—Delagoa Fares.—Explorers', Tourists', and Gold Prospectors' Outfits.—Getting an Expedition together.—Purchase and Fittings of Waggon.—Cattle, how to Choose them.—Servants, Pay and Treatment.—Hours for Travelling.—Marches.—Details.—Halts.—Tulip.—Treatment of Cattle in Sickness.—Provisions.—Medicines.—Treatment of Sickness and Wounds in Men.—Dysentery.—Fever.—Wounds.—Ulcers.—Snakebite.—Fuel.—A Journey on Foot.—Bearers.—How to make a Raft.—Kite principle of Delivering Supplies 181

CHAPTER XXIV

How to get to SOUTH AFRICA—Outfit—History of the UNION STEAM SHIP COMPANY.

PAGE.

Uncertainty of past times removed.—Facilities for Information.—Outfit.—Safety of Ocean Voyages compared to Railway Train Travelling.—History of the Union Steam Ship Company.—List of Fleet and Tonnage.—Records of Speed.—The Services.—The Voyage to the Cape.—General Information for Passengers ... 189

APPENDICES.

Native Words and Phrases.—Latitudes.—Longitudes.—Altitudes.—Weather Signs.—Atlantic Distances.—African Distances.—Nearest Ports.—Modes of Conveyance.—Routes and Fares to Transvaal Gold Fields.—Directors of the Union Steam Ship Co.—Offices and Agencies 199

LIST OF ILLUSTRATIONS xv

LIST OF ILLUSTRATIONS.

Cape Town and Table Bay	to face page	1
Adderley Street, Cape Town	,, ,,	15
Port Elizabeth	,, ,,	19
East London	,, ,,	21
Kimberley (Mine and Town)	,, ,,	31
Town Hall, Durban, Natal	,, ,,	53
A Street in Durban	,, ,,	59
Crossing a Drift (Road to Umzinto, Natal)	,, ,,	77
Eland's Spruit (Road to Barberton)	,, ,,	129
Johannesburg (Panoramic View)	,, ,,	133
Zulu Boys	,, ,,	155
Delagoa Bay	,, ,,	175
Steam Ship "Tartar"	,, ,,	189
Map of South Africa	end of book.	

	PAGE.
View of Cape Town (Vignette)	12
Fingoes at Home	15
View on St. John's River	34
Native Gold Fields, Tugela River	67
Umzimvubu River	72
Lions	111
Post and Passenger Car to Gold Fields	133
Opening a Reef in Witwatersrandt Gold Fields	140
A Zulu Warrior	146
A Zulu Prophetess (Vignette)	151
Zulu Village or Kraal	153
A Zulu Chief	156
Darker Buck	158
Royal Kraal or Great Place, Swazieland	167
Dead Zebra	169
Dead Buffalo	173

CAPE TOWN AND TABLE BAY.

(*From a Photograph by Robert Harris.*)

CHAPTER I.

A SHORT ACCOUNT OF THE DISCOVERY AND COLONISATION OF THE CAPE COLONY, BY THE PORTUGUESE, DUTCH, AND ENGLISH.

THE weird tales of adventure which have been put forth from time to time regarding Africa, have succeeded in drawing such a veil of mystery over the country, that the ordinary reader has come to regard it as a region where savage and unapproachable nations live and die in a miserable state of perpetual bloodshed, strife, superstition and bondage. Sandy deserts, like unhealthy dreams, pass before his mind, and horrible rites as practised by the natives cause him to turn from the subject with feelings closely akin to loathing. Those who follow me through these pages, however, will speedily learn how erroneous and unjust such impressions are. True it is, that in certain localities some such horrors as those enumerated do occur occasionally, but they are not nearly so common or general as one might infer from the accounts of romantic and imaginative writers, who have found in Africa that convenient uncertainty so necessary to the success of their productions. It will be my task to glance briefly and comprehensively at British, Dutch and Portuguese Africa, and then plunge with my readers into the wilder and little known, but none the less fertile regions inland, where primitive man still reigns as happily as ever did our original ancestors by the far Euphrates. I do not aim merely at writing a guide book, but rather at painting a faithful picture of the great land that is, in my opinion, destined in the very early future to dazzle the world with the magnitude of its hidden treasures and to add another empire, pregnant with resources, to our already grand and glorious one.

It must not be imagined that this desirable result will ever be fully attained without earnest and fearless endeavour on the part of Imperial citizens and Colonial pioneers, who must combine to unravel the many problems that inevitably beset the construction of a new land; and if a word or a line from my pen should chance either to encourage or aid the good work, I shall feel in a sense rewarded for the years of hardship and labour which I have spent amongst the dusky natives, who to-day stand watching the advance of that civilisation which means either a renewal of life or a war of extermination to them. Time and again the trembling balance has tended, within the past twenty years, to the latter terrible contingency; but, happily, the war-wave spent itself before it roused the hot, eager blood of those who dwell "beyond the Zulus." It is the mission—nay, the bounden duty—of every traveller, be he simple tourist or professional explorer, to strain every nerve in the work of conciliation for the double purpose of preserving some of the noble tribes of Africa, who, as will be shown presently, are well worthy to stand shoulder to shoulder with us, and to secure a field for the constantly increasing population of the great centres of the homeland.

The world is, so to speak, daily growing smaller. Far out and almost unheard of regions are now, owing to a constant and perfect system of ocean steam navigation, brought within negotiable distance. To set out for Africa is no longer

The Union Steam Ship Company, Limited.

a task of severe self-sacrifice; and to settle in that country is far removed from the species of exile that it used to be. The question as to whether Africa would ever become a useful producing country is now, I think, admitted by the world to have received a final and grand answer. The fact that the Diamond Mines have added six tons weight of diamonds, with a value of £39,000,000 to the wealth of the world; that within the past twenty-five years *one thousand tons* of ostrich feathers have been shipped from the Cape, and that the newly-discovered Gold Fields are daily and hourly pouring forth their golden grains, speaks for itself.

All this may savour somewhat of boastfulness, for Africa is so much my country that, like a fond mother, I am apt to revel in her rapidly increasing glory; yet an examination of statistics will prove the accuracy of my statements, which are not excessive when it is remembered that I have not mentioned other valuable productions, such as wool, tea, arrowroot, hides, horns, ivory, and half-a-hundred other necessaries of civilisation.

Having thus outlined something of the wealth of the country, we will turn to the story of the discovery of its southern extremities, and learn something of the brave hearts whose labours still echo through the " corridors of Time."

The records of early African exploration are brimful of interest to the student of history. There is a chivalry, a romance and a fascination about them far exceeding that of other lands. Glancing back, we find that in the year 1415, this fascination still hung over the land of gold and ivory. For King John the First of Portugal having heard of the wonderful reported wealth of the African sultans and kings, fitted out armies under able generals and sent them forth with the intent to wrest some of their gold from them, for the " Glory of God and Portugal."

The accounts left by these primitive explorers form a distinct literature, while their maps and charts are veritable works of art. Gilded domes set with rich gems; vast and populous cities, stately and grand almost beyond conception, were cast here, there, and everywhere with a lavish hand; while monsters of unspeakable ferocity barred their path and threatened them with instant death. Unicorns were everyday occurrences; wild men of the woods fought side by side with golden helmeted Amazons, of most dangerous and seductive beauty; while strange rumbling sounds and fiery mountains came in just where required. I have travelled over the same ground, and looked in vain for some of these horrors, but never an Amazon with any pretension to beauty could I find.

Whether these navigators told their stories in good faith, or for the purpose of enhancing their achievements, I will not say, for it is ill work to slander dead men; but simple justice requires that we should give them honour, for they dared grandly and died right loyally in the effort to glorify their nation and build up her power. Divested of all the romance lent by untutored minds, their labours stand to-day as a monument to valour and an example to us of a more enlightened age.

Those who have toiled through the African wilds, even with our modern appliances and comforts, know what privation means; but what must it have been to them as, clad in cumbersome armour, they struggled on and on into the unknown and the mysterious? Overhead, the sun, like a shield of fire, poured down his rays on them, while on one hand a lonely sea, and on the other, the fierce untamed natives spake only of torment, solitude or death. I have often pictured, while on my own travels, the terrible reality of the brave King Sebastian's toils, when, followed by a throng of champions, he set out on the conquest of Africa—no small task. They landed, it is said, in the very heart of the fever king's realm, described by a poet as a region

> Where plains of quaking sand roll up in waves,
> And unnamed rivers flow past meadow lands;
> Where never man is seen, and frightful beasts
> Make the night hideous with hoarse bellowings.—*Odean.*

The Union Steam Ship Company, Limited.

At first all went well with them, for they were accredited by the natives with supernatural powers and attributes, but not for long; the whistling arrows and the heavy clubs soon set to work and stretched many a brave cavalier on the alien soil. Slowly but surely the end came on; visions of conquest and wealth vanished like morning vapours, and the terrible reality of defeat and death stared the survivors in the face. Provisions expended, pestilence gnawing into their very hearts—how they must have longed for a glimpse of their native land; and how they must have strained their eyes over the lonely sea in search of a sail that never came. Still, on and on, until wearied to death, they sank, one by one, and died raving in delirium and beating their breasts in hopelessness. Surely we cannot wonder that the romancers have seized on the land, and, ignoring its own inherent worth, have dashed it with the poetry and the pathos of death.

Much, if not all this distress and suffering was begotten of ignorance of the climatic requirements of the region, and of an utter lack of that conciliatory policy which cannot be too earnestly inculcated. Modern travellers have since found that even in the most deadly fever regions, care and foresight will do much to lessen, if not remove, the danger of infection; while the dusky potentates, who have been described as unapproachable, are in reality anything but bad fellows, when properly treated. I have, on more than one occasion, clasped hands with some of them in firm friendship and brotherhood.

Passing from the epoch of uncertainty, we find that later in the same century (1486), that indefatigable navigator, Bartholomew Diaz, sailed round the Cape, and changed its name from "Cabo Tormentoso" to the more promising and prophetic one of "Cabo de Boa Esperança." Eleven years later, Vasco de Gama followed him to that region, and, heading north along the East Coast, truthfully, carefully, and well, explored and described the region now known as Natal, which was so called from the fact of its discovery on Christmas

Day (1497). Passing on, he added to the geographical knowledge of the world by exploring Delagoa Bay, Inhambane, Quilimane and Mozambique.

It was not to be expected that these explorers—with their primitive galleys, restricted appliances, and necessarily small force—should do much in the way of inland exploration; that was a question for the very distant future, for we find that for about two hundred years the field of their labours lay almost fallow.

The harbours only, it appears, were visited at long intervals by occasional navigators who sought shelter in them from stress of weather: of these, Table Bay and Saldanha Bay were the most favoured; and we read of how the commanders (named Shillinge and Fitz-Herbert) of a small English fleet landed and took possession of the South African Coast in the name of His Majesty King James the First. As far as history goes that was the end of the matter, and the Hottentots, who at that time were a fine robust nation, held on their way in happy carelessness of the world beyond their magic and shipless waters.

In the beginning of the seventeenth century a company of Dutch merchants obtained a Charter from the States General of the United Provinces, and set about establishing a Trading Station in the vicinity of the present Cape Town. At this time the Hottentots, of whom mention has already been made, were ruled over by a paramount chief or king called Manckhagon, who, in consideration of the value of four thousand reals of Eight in sundry goods and articles, sold to the Dutchmen a district extending from Lion Hill (of which more anon) along the Coast of Table Bay, with the Hout and Saldanha Bays inclusive. The Governor, if we may so term him, of this germ of a colony, was named Jan Anthony Van Riebeek, a surgeon by profession, and a good, straightforward man by nature. A few years later he concluded another purchase, from a chief named Dhouw. This latter acquisition included False Bay and its adjacent cape, so that even thus early we find civilisation widening and taking a firmer grip on the land.

It must not be imagined that this meant anything like a robbery of the natives, for the land really represented no value to them, and its occupation by the burly, phlegmatic and good-humoured settlers was a distinct advantage, for markets were established where they might exchange their cattle and such vegetables as they cared to raise for the necessaries and luxuries imported or produced by the whites. According to history, the most friendly and cordial relations existed between the two races.

Although Van Riebeek was such a painstaking and conscientious ruler, he does not seem to have been either ambitious or progressive, for he made, as far as I can learn, no attempt to increase the settlement or elevate it to the dignity of a "Colony," as we understand the word. That task was reserved for a successor, named Simon van der Stell. This astute personage seems to have been the first to realise that although the Cape of Good Hope was not Holland, and home, yet that it more than matched it in fertility and wealth. The Directors of the Company, on his representations, resolved to send out a number of agriculturists, who were to obtain land-grants.

Mr. John Noble, in his interesting history of *South Africa*, tells us that, at this period, the religious persecution of the Protestants, set on foot by the revocation of the Edict of Nantes, was flooding the Dutch Republic with refugee Waldenses from Piedmont and the Italian Alps. The Dutchmen received and sheltered them in a thorough spirit of Christianity and brotherhood. As many of these refugees were "persons who understood the culture of the vine and were willing and anxious to emigrate," Van Stell's want was soon supplied and that with just the right sort of men. I will ask you to note the origin here of these folk, for later on, when we find ourselves journeying amongst their direct descendants, the present "Boers," or farmers, it will be interesting to note the resemblance between the old stock and their present stalwart representatives.

The terms of their settlement were liberal and kindly to the last degree, for referring to Mr. Noble's history again, we learn that "Those applying themselves to farming should be given as much ground as they could bring under cultivation; and, in case of requiring it, should be furnished with all implements necessary and even seed, upon condition that they should afterwards re-imburse the Company for such advances, in corn, wine or other goods." Over one hundred and fifty men, women, and children, were introduced under these auspices, and, be it noted, with the happiest results.

Although matters were progressing in a placid and peaceful manner, the people were not without a grievance, for the Company possessed a monopoly of trade, and exclusive authority over the sale of produce. The first cloud that arose in the horizon of this primitive and out-of-the-way settlement, was the outcome of this monopoly, against which a memorial was framed and forwarded home. As soon as Stell discovered this, he imprisoned or exiled the ringleaders, and thundered his wrath in proclamations against the others. But discontent must find a vent, and the vent in this case was a gradual dispersion of the settlers towards the interior of the country, where some of them, it was feared, stood in danger of lapsing into barbarism by reason of the wildness of their surroundings.

In order to avert this, the authorities at the Cape established a magistracy at Swellendam, and appointed a minister of religion to whip in those whose eyes were wandering to the strange women of the native tribes. Fortunately but little, if any, intermarriage took place, otherwise a serious check might have been given to the civilisation of the country. Steadily as they advanced, the colonists, settlers, squatters, or whatever they might be called, displaced the complaisant Hottentots; but met with difficulty from the Bushmen who inhabited the hills, now known as the Roggveld, Nieuweld and the

The Union Steam Ship Company, Limited.

Sneuwbergen; while the warlike Kafirs in the east and north-east checked their spread in those regions.

In consequence of these two hostile elements, the farmers, on the outskirts of the flying fringe of civilisation, were often in great peril. The Kafirs began to fear that they, like the Hottentots, were to be displaced by the "White-ones," and the ready spears were lifted in defiance. This had a good effect on the colonists, for it made them value what they had, and cease to covet that of others. The necessity for combination for purposes of defence had now arisen, and from it sprang the system now known in the present Republics as the "Commando." Rough and ready leaders, called "Veld Cornets," were elected; these acted as captains and organisers in the event of any outbreak or disturbance.

We will now leave the interior provinces and take a peep at the coast again, where matters began to assume rather an unpleasant aspect, for (1782) war had broken out between England and Holland. The latter country, having enough for her soldiers to do at home, could spare none for the defence of the Cape. The supply of money was also stopped, and the establishment of a paper currency was the result. This currency speedily fell in value, and great discontent broke out amongst the settlers. While some went into open revolt, others, of the better sort, took more constitutional means to obtain a reform of the whole code of laws—notably those which governed and cramped trade. Just at this juncture, as though their own internal troubles were not enough, a foe, in the form of an English fleet under Admiral Stephenstone and General Craig, appeared off the Cape.

It seems that in Europe an alliance had been entered into between the Prince of Orange (who had found a refuge in England) and the English, against their common enemy—France. The English being fully alive to the importance of the Cape as a port of call on the Indian route, despatched this fleet to hold the post. General Craig bore with him a letter from the Prince of Orange to his "good people." But the aforesaid good people regarded the epistle of the refugee William with anything but respect, and refused to allow the British forces to land. Marshalling their little army, which numbered about one thousand whites and three thousand blacks, under able and brave officers, they prepared to do battle. Forts were thrown up near Kalk Bay (where their remains may still be seen), and the dogs of war were loosed. After a gallant fight, in which two of the colonial officers greatly distinguished themselves, a halt was called, and negotiations entered into, with the result that the English entered Cape Town.

Thus ended the existence of the Dutch Company's power in Africa.

I will bring the early records of the country to a close as speedily as possible; but, in order to thoroughly grasp the situation, it is necessary to record the fact, that General Craig, having assumed the reins of government, proclaimed Free Trade, and other reforms: such as restoring to its value the paper currency, introducing a fresh supply of specie, and establishing tribunals of justice. Affairs were shaping well, when (1802) in accordance with the treaty of Amiens, which had been executed the previous year, the region was restored to the Hollanders, but only for a time. A governor, named Janssens, was appointed, and an honest attempt made to establish a firm and prosperous possession. Considerable difficulty was experienced in ruling the frontier farmers, who, during these changes, were leading a roisterous and independent life. Forming in gangs, like the Moss Troopers of old between England and Scotland, they lived almost entirely by the plunder they took from the Kafirs, while those dusky and wily braves, not to be outdone, waged a return war on the Whites. The governor divided the country into five counties or districts, *i.e.*, Stellenbosch, Swellendam, Graaff Reinet, Uitenhage, and Tulbagh. Magistrates (called landdrosts) were appointed, and some show of force made, in order to remove the farmers' excuse that " they were obliged, in self defence, to loot the natives." Under this *régime* much good was done, but it was reserved for the English to do the real work of civilisation. War was again declared in Europe (1805), and a British expedition set sail for the purpose of holding the Cape, as before. After some fighting, in which both the English and Dutch warriors distinguished themselves for bravery and devotion, victory declared itself on the side of the British. The Batavian troops fell back, under Janssens, who, in response to an appeal from Sir David Baird, the English general, came to terms, and embarked for Holland. Even at this period the British Government was not alive to the wealth and importance of the Cape and adjacent territories as a colony, regarding it merely in the light of a military and naval post.

Following Sir David Baird, came the Earl of Caledon and Sir John Cradock, who did much, by the kindliness and policy of their behaviour, to cement good fellowship between the settlers, who were for the most part of the old stock. New blood was sadly needed, and the introduction of colonists clamoured for. In order to show how this took place, I cannot do better than quote the following paragraph from Mr. Noble's history of South Africa, which is an invaluable book to all who desire to take an intelligent interest in the development of the country.

"Shortly after the close of the war with Napoleon the First, when trade was oppressed and emigration was looked upon as an outlet for the relief of the unemployed, the British Parliament voted £50,000 towards colonising the country. In a short time, 90,000 applications for passages were sent in, although only 4,000 could be accepted. Most of these emigrants were landed at Algoa Bay, in 1820. These may be looked upon as the 'Pilgrim Fathers' of Africa. The Rev. Mr. Dugmore, a son of one of the earliest settlers, has preserved to us his recollections of their arrival and the spots where they were located. Bailie's party, he says, made their way to the mouth of the Fish River; Wilson's party settled on the plains of the Waaiplaats and the Kowie Bush—right across the path of the elephants, some of which they tried to shoot with fowling-pieces; while Sefton's party founded the village of Salem."

And so it went on; smaller groups dotted the intervals between the larger ones, each forming centres, which have since grown to stately dimensions. One unpleasant episode, which had an important bearing on the extension of colonisation, occurred about this period (1835-6). Owing to the imperfect knowledge of the natives possessed by the newly-established English authorities, considerable injustice, it is said, was done to certain of the Dutch frontier communities, who, after protesting in vain against the native policy which was being carried out, resolved to strike off to the northward and establish for themselves an independent state.

These adventurers will be dealt with at a later stage of the story. Meanwhile, there is a great temptation to follow in detail the labours of the brave and enterprising settlers who remained in spite of discouragements and dangers. How they fought and toiled, and cheerfully endured, is all set down in other works. Suffice it for us that they lived and thrived, despite their adverse circumstances, and from the seeds sown by them we have a prosperous and rich dependency, worthy in every respect of the great nations from which it has sprung. Leaving history now, we will take a peep at the Cape Colony as it is, and then resume our journey, for we have much ground to travel over.

CHAPTER II.

THE CAPE COLONY OF TO-DAY.

THE superficial area of the Cape Colony is 213,636 miles, or about double the size of the whole of Great Britain and Ireland.

It is bounded on the east by the Umtata River, from its mouth to the town of Umtata, and from thence along the line of road separating Griqualand East from Pondoland to a point on the Umtamvuna River, touching the boundary of Natal. Thence to the Umzinkulu River, and north to the Drakensberg range of mountains, following them to the source of the Telle River and thence to its junction with the Orange River and along the course of this natural boundary to a point named Ramah, then in a northerly direction along the frontier of the Orange Free State to Platberg on the Vaal River, thence following that stream to its junction with the Orange River, and on to the sea on the West Coast. The population of the Colony is computed at present at 1,252,347, made up of all nations—well leavened with English and Dutch.

The first glimpse of the Cape Peninsula which the voyager obtains, presents a characteristic specimen of the form and structure of the mountain ranges of the country. It would require the inspired pencil of a Doré, and the majestic measures of a Milton to do full justice to the vastness and beauty of the great "Table Mountain" that rises in abrupt cliffs from the sea to an altitude of 3,852 feet. The clouds almost continually hover about its towering crests, which suggest the idea of an altar worthy of the Master at whose command they took form.

Nestling on the lower slopes of the mountain lies the metropolis of South Africa, which at first sight, owing to the magnitude of its surroundings, does not impress one with its dimensions. The mountain itself is flanked on the right by a curious-looking hill called the Lion's Head, which attains 2,000 feet or more of altitude. The continuation of this hill supplies the rest of the body of the "King of Beasts." The Devil's Peak towers on the left. This hill was called "Windberg" by the ancient navigators. It lifts its head to an elevation of 3,315 feet, and it is in the semicircular valley between this latter and the great central mountain that Cape Town is built. The delicate tinting of the rocks, and the luxuriant foliage which clothes their lower reaches, particularly, imparts a charm to the scenery, which is especially welcome after the sea voyage.

On landing, the visitor will be pleasantly surprised to find that he has not, in crossing the ocean, left either home life or home associations behind him. Jostling each other on the wharves and in the streets are to be seen a busy throng of toilers, each as earnestly "focused" on winning the almighty dollar as even the heart of the most captious advocate of civilisation and progress could desire. The brown, yellow and black hue of some of those who first meet the eye is pleasantly relieved by the homely visages of the English, Irish, and Scotch colonists, whose tongues lend themselves to all languages; for one may hear all sorts of barbarous lingoes spoken with a fine Scottish accent, or with a rollicking Irish brogue. The streets are broad and straight, having been laid out after the Dutch style; while the houses, many of which are flat-roofed, are substantial, stately, and well abreast of the times. The main thoroughfare, Adderley Street, would do no discredit to an

ADDERLEY STREET, CAPE TOWN.
(From a Photograph by Robert Harris.)

English provincial city, while here and there one comes unexpectedly on an architectural pile of great beauty.

The climate of the town, though hot in summer, is pleasant, and for health is remarkably good. Hitherto, some complaints have been made, and with justice, touching sanitary arrangements; but this defect is rapidly being removed, and doubtless by the time these pages see the light, will have been altogether remedied. Amongst the public buildings of note we may mention the Houses of Parliament, which were erected at a cost of £220,000, and the Standard Bank, which cost £32,000.

There is no lack of good hotels, clubs and boarding houses to suit all classes of visitors and settlers, while rents are fair and in proportion to the scale of wages. One may live as economically there as in England, and if desired, every requisite in the way of luxury is within call. Provisions and food are reasonable in price.

Turning from the features of Cape Town to its inhabitants, we glean from the latest statistics that the population is estimated at 62,000 souls. This comprises white and coloured races; of the latter, specimens of many kinds are to be seen, Malays, Fingoes, Bushmen, Indians, Kafirs, Half-castes, &c.,

Fingoes at Home.

&c., from pale sickly yellow, to a deep, funereal, and unmistakable black. Society of a most enjoyable and cultivated description is to be had, but the intending tourist or settler will do well to provide himself with letters of introduction and other credentials, for without these, "None shall enter." This may at first appear to be an exclusive and tyrannical rule, but nevertheless it is a necessary one; and to it may be traced the freedom from reserve, and the complete kindliness of the colonists to those who are admitted to their circles. The idea that, because colonists are colonists they must necessarily be either uncouth or untutored, is a theory that has been given up long ago.

In glancing over a modern map of the Cape Colony, on which all the towns, villages and hamlets are set down, the eye is almost confused by their number, and for a moment it is hard to believe that the place has, in truth, advanced so marvellously within the past thirty years, for prior to that time, little attention was, as I have striven to show, devoted to the real development of the country. There are now seven provinces, which, for magisterial and fiscal convenience, are sub-divided into seventy divisions or districts as follows :—

Western Province.

Divisions and Districts.	Towns and Villages.
Cape Town	Cape Town and Green Point.
Cape Division, Wynberg, Simon's Town.	Woodstock, Maitland, Mowbray, Rondebosch, Newlands, Claremont, Kenilworth, Wynberg, Constantia, Muizenberg, Kalk Bay, Simon's Town, Kuil's River, Blueberg, and Durban.
Stellenbosch	Stellenbosch, Eerste River, Somerset West, and the Strand.
Paarl	Paarl, Wellington, Drakenstein, Frenchhoek.

North-Western Province.

Malmesbury	Malmesbury, Darling, Hopefield, St. Helena Bay, Riebeck West, Mamre, Groenekloof.
Piquetberg	Piquetberg, Porterville, and Goedverwacht.
Namaqualand, Port Nolloth.	Springbokfontein, Hondeklip Bay, Port Nolloth, Bowesdorp, and Leliefontein.
Clanwilliam	Clanwilliam, Troe Troe, Calvinia, Brandvley, and Katkop.
Worcester, Tulbagh, Ceres.	Worcester, Ceres, Tulbagh, Steinthal, Gouda, Bergville, Hermon, Wolseley, and Prince Alfred.

The Union Steam Ship Company, Limited.

South-Western Province.

Divisions and Districts.	Towns and Villages.
Swellendam, Robertson	Swellendam, Heidelberg, Zuurbraak, Malagas, Port Beaufort, Robertson, Montagu, and Lady Grey.
Riversdale, Ladysmith.	Riversdale, Ladysmith, and Amalienstein.
Caledon, Bredasdorp.	Caledon Genadendal, Villiersdorp, Greyton, Bredasdorp, Elim, and Napier.
Oudtshoorn	Oudtshoorn, Cango, and Calitzdorp.
George, Uniondale, Mossel Bay, Knysna.	George, Blanco, Hopedale, Uniondale, Schoonberg, Pacaltsdorp, Lyon, Aliwal South, Plettenberg's Bay, Melville, Belvidere, Newhaven, Redbourne, and Edmundton.

Midland Province.

Graaff Reinet, Murraysburg, Aberdeen.	Graaff Reinet, Petersburg, Aberdeen and Murraysberg.
Beaufort, Prince Albert, Willowmore.	Beaufort, Prince Albert, Petersburg, Willowmore.
Victoria West, Prieska, Fraserburg, Sutherland, Carnarvon.	Victoria West, Prieska, Fraserburg, Ondersto, Doorns, Kenhardt, Upington, Sutherland, and Carnarvon.
Richmond, Hope Town.	Richmond, Britz Town, and Hope Town.

South-Eastern Province.

Albany, Bathurst.	Graham's Town, Salem, Sidbury, Riebeek, Bathurst, Port Frances, and Port Alfred.
Victoria East, Peddie.	Alice, Aberdeen, and Peddie.
Uitenhage, Jansenville, Humansdorp, Alexandria.	Uitenhage, Jansenville, Humansdorp, Hankey, Alexandria, Paterson.
Port Elizabeth	Port Elizabeth, Zwartkops, and Walmer.

North-Eastern Province.

Fort Beaufort, Stockenstrom.	Fort Beaufort, Post Retief, Adelaide, Heald Town, Elands Post (Seymour), Hertzog, Balfour, and Philip Town.

North-Eastern Province—continued.

Divisions and Districts.	Towns and Villages.
Albert	Burghersdorp, Molteno, Sterkstroom, and Ventersburg.
Somerset East. Bedford.	Somerset East, Groote Vlakte, Been Leegte, Pearston, Bedford, and Glenlynden.
Cradock. Steynsburg.	Cradock, Steynsburg, and Maraisburg.
Colesberg. Hanover. Middelburg.	Colesberg, Philipstown, Hanover, and Middelburg.

Eastern Province.

King William's Town. Stutterheim. Komgha.	King William's Town, Berlin, Breidbach, Braunsweigh, Frankfort, Stutterheim, and Komgha.
East London	East London, Panmure, Potsdam, and Maclean.
Queen's Town. Cathcart. Tarka.	Queen's Town, Whittlesea, Tarkastad, Lady Frere, Glen Grey, and Cathcart.
Aliwal North. Herschel.	Aliwal North, Lady Grey, James Town, and Herschel.
Wodehouse. Barkly East.	Dordrecht and Barkly East.

Griqualand West Province.

Kimberley. Herbert. Barkly West. Upper Hay.	Kimberley, De Beer's, Beaconsfield, Du Toit's Pan, Herbert, Barkly West, Pniel, Douglas and Griqua Town.

Transkeian Territories and Griqualand East.

Butterworth, Umtata, Kokstad.

In a general work such as the present, it would be an impossible task to attempt anything like a detailed description of the above enumerated settlements; suffice it to say, that they are all cleanly and habitable, each possessing its own institutions and its own attractions. There is, as a rule, a great similarity about these villages and towns, and there is not such a vast difference as one would suppose between village or inland town life in the Cape and in England. At frequent intervals English and Continental Mails are delivered; and the affairs of the great outside world are as earnestly and as intelli-

PORT ELIZABETH.

(*From a Photograph by Robert Harris.*)

gently discussed round the fireside and in the tavern, as in any hamlet of the homeland. Many, if not all these centres, have their daily and weekly papers, while local elections and domestic intelligence serve to keep the gossips as lively and as happy as is desirable.

The Cape Colony is particularly well supplied by Nature with harbours. All along the coast, from the mouth of the Orange River on the west coast, to Pondoland (St. John's River) on the south-east coast, commodious havens are to be found; some of them are already well advanced by public enterprise and professional skill, others are by Nature fitted with all necessary requirements, and others again but await the expenditure of a few thousands, to render them of national importance. In Table Bay a large and commodious dock has been erected and was opened by H.R.H. Prince Alfred, in 1869 or 1870. In order to carry out repairs on large vessels a graving dock was constructed and opened in 1882 by Sir H. Robinson, the governor, after whom it is named.

Simon's Bay, which is situated near Table Bay, is the naval station for H.M.'s ships. There is a neat little seaport town there where ships may be provisioned and repairs carried out. The country in the vicinity is as picturesque and healthy as the rest of the Colony. Mossel Bay, which is half way between Cape Town and Algoa Bay, is, from its position, a port of considerable importance, being the *entrepôt* for the central coast districts of the Colony. Algoa Bay is the main harbour for the midland and eastern districts. It is an open roadstead, but has good holding ground. Owing to the surf, vessels cannot come close inshore, but the discharge of cargoes is expeditiously carried out by means of steam tugs. The town of Port Elizabeth, which has sprung up on the shore of Algoa Bay, is one of considerable importance; in fact, it may be classed as one of the principal commercial centres of the Colony. It is connected by rail with Kimberley, Uitenhage, Graham's Town, Graaff Reinet and Colesberg. It extends for two or three miles along the shore and has invaded the hill to the westward.

The style of architecture is all that can be desired, while its sanitary arrangements, and consequent good health, are highly spoken of. It has a population of about 18,000, principally Whites, and forms the seaport for a vast extent of inland territory. Living expenses in Port Elizabeth are very similar to Cape Town; and, I may say here, that the same applies throughout British South Africa. A frugal traveller may live on an advance, say, of 15 per cent., on his expenditure in England. Travelling is, of course, more costly in proportion, as a study of the tables of fares in the Appendix will show. But this is to be expected when the number of tourists is so small. Within the past ten years a very visible reduction has been made, and each year will see matters still further levelled to the English scale.

Port Alfred, which is situated at the mouth of the Kowie River, has good holding ground for ships, which, however, if over a certain tonnage, cannot as yet enter the inner harbour or lagoon.

A steam tug and lighter are always in attendance, as at Algoa Bay, and landing and shipping are carried out with despatch.

About a mile up stream there are wharves and depôts, while the railway to Graham's Town connects with the port, and thereby imparts to it an additional importance.

East London, at the mouth of the Buffalo River, is the next harbour of note, where works under Sir John Coode have been in progress. The purpose of these operations is to remove the sand bar from the river's mouth and secure an entrance to the deep water inside the barrier. The dredger, which has now been at work for some time, has effected this purpose in a great measure, and, as a consequence, the commerce of East London has considerably increased. Although the harbours which have been mentioned are only a small proportion of those which will be developed as the country progresses, enough has been said to prove that, as a maritime region, the Cape Colony is second to none. Her chief defect in this

EAST LONDON.

(*From a Photograph by Robert Harris.*)

direction arises from the fact that but few of the rivers or inlets of the sea are navigable for any considerable distance.

The railway system of the colony is, considering all things, in a most advanced and prosperous condition. There are three main systems, *i.e.*, the Western, the Midland, and the Eastern. The first mentioned starts from Cape Town, and traverses a distance of over 500 miles, touching at Beaufort West, thence to De Aar Junction, where it is joined by the Midland system, and thence on to Kimberley Diamond Fields, thereby covering a distance of 647 miles from Cape Town. Branches spring from the first-mentioned system, which touch Malmsbury, Wynberg, and Stellenbosch. The Midland system starts from Algoa Bay (Port Elizabeth) in three separate branches, viz., (1) To Graaff Reinet, 185 miles. (2) To Cradock, 182 miles; Middelburg Road, 243 miles; Colesberg, 308 miles; De Aar Junction, 338 miles, where it joins the Western system, as above stated, and goes on to Kimberley, 484 miles. And (3) to Graham's Town, 106 miles, with many intermediate stations. The Eastern system starts from East London and runs to Queenstown, 154 miles; Sterkstroom, 190 miles; Burgersdorp, 244 miles; and now touches Aliwal North, 280 miles, this being the terminus of the system. A branch runs to King William's Town, 42 miles from East London. A private line has been started by a company, from Graham's Town to Port Alfred, 43 miles, and is now opened throughout.

Before passing to other matters it may be well to state that the most direct route to Kimberley, the chief centre of the Diamond Fields, is from Cape Town, by rail throughout, a distance, as already mentioned, of 647 miles. An express train leaves Cape Town at 1.15 p.m. every Thursday, conveying first-class passengers through to Kimberley, and arriving there at 9 p.m. on the following day. A return express train leaves Kimberley at 5 a.m. every Tuesday and Saturday, arriving at Cape Town at 12.30 p.m. next day. An ordinary train, each way, leaves daily (Sundays excepted), and conveys passengers of all classes. The fares on this line are:—From Cape Town to Kimberley, 1st class, £8 1s. 9d.; 2nd class, £5 7s. 10d.; 3rd class, £2 13s. 11d. The free allowance of luggage to each passenger being 100 lb., 50 lb. and 25 lb., according to class. These fares are, of course, liable to alteration. The journey from Port Elizabeth to Kimberley may also be done by rail throughout, the distance being 485 miles. A fast train leaves the Port every Monday, conveying first-class passengers, and arriving at Kimberley at 9.35 p.m. next day. A return train leaves Kimberley every *Saturday* at 5 p.m., arriving in the Port at 6.40 a.m. on *Sunday*. An ordinary train (each way) daily conveys passengers of all classes. The fares from Port Elizabeth to Kimberley are:—1st class, £6 1s. 3d.; 2nd class, £4 0s. 10d.; 3rd class, £2 0s. 5½d. Free allowances for passengers' luggage are similar to those on the Cape Town line. These fares also are liable to alteration, as are the arrivals and departures of the trains. Accidents on the Cape Colony railways are of extreme rarity, great care being exercised in the selection and appointment of officials. The rolling stock is exactly similar to that of an English line, while the travelling is as comfortable. At most of the stations, refreshment bars are provided, where the usual and historic sandwich, or hard-boiled egg, may be indulged in.

The produce of the Cape Colony presents a feature of absorbing interest to every intelligent visitor. Since a very early period in the Colonial history, wool has taken an important place. We learn from published statistics that in the year 1831, the total quantity of wool imported into the United Kingdom from English colonies, was 11,859 bales. In 1884, the imports from the Cape and Australia amounted to 1,273,732 bales. The total of the fifty-five years gives the grand amount of 21,322,592 bales, representing a value of £421,121,192.

By these figures, it will be seen that the Cape Colony, and adjacent territories, are well adapted to the requirements of the sheep farmer.

Ostrich feathers form another of the Cape's principal exports. While the birds from which the feathers were collected were only to be found in a wild state, and obtained after long and tedious hunting, it is not to be wondered at that the export was inconsiderable. This difficulty was overcome by Mr. A. Douglas, of Heatherton, who, by his adaptation of the "Incubator" to the requirements of ostrich eggs, succeeded in hatching and rearing the birds. Owing to this most valuable departure, the export in 1870 rose to 28,786 lb., valued at £91,229. After this encouragement the industry rapidly developed. In 1875 a census was taken of the Cape Colony, and the return showed a total of 21,751 birds, as against 80 at the beginning of the decade; and so it went on increasing until, in 1882, which was an exceptionally successful year, the exports amounted to 253,954 lb., valued at £1,093,989.

Raw materials form the staple of the exports; but a considerable amount of labour and capital is employed in manufactures for local consumption. The production of wine, brewing of beer, and distillation of spirits, are recognised industries. In the vicinity of Cape Town there are seven or eight breweries; while in certain districts the cultivation of hops is being successfully carried on.

Cabinet making, waggon and carriage building, tailoring and shoemaking, iron-founding and engineering, are to be classed amongst the important industries of the country. Soap making, biscuit baking by machinery, and the production of all sorts of jams and jellies from the rich and varied fruit-supply of the region, are also regarded as promising arenas for the enterprise and energy of the colonists. Guano islands occur off the coast, and give occupation to about 400 boats and 2,000 persons; while the quantity and value of the cured fish exported in 1884 was 2,741,966 lbs., worth £16,206. Salt-pans also occur in many of the divisions, and great quantities of that commodity are annually produced.

It will be remembered that, in sketching the early colonisation of the Cape, mention was made of the introduction of certain refugee emigrants from the banks of the Rhine, who were learned in the culture of the grape. These settlers produced their first vintage in 1659. The industry went on steadily increasing until, in 1880, the statistical returns of the vineyards show that there were about 60,000,000 vines in the colony. This has increased by over a million since that year. As a technical treatment of the subject would be out of place in this handbook, I will content myself by enumerating the kinds of grapes which thrive there. According to Baron Von Babo, the principal are—

1. The Common Green Grape.
2. The Hannepool.
3. The Stein Grape.
4. Red Muscadel.
5. White Muscadel.

In addition to wine—brandy, raisins, and the fruit themselves are extensively exported. The amount of land under vines is computed to be about 21,000 acres.

In 1872, the Cape Colony obtained the boon (?) of Responsible Government, though the Crown has still the sole right of appointing Governors and of exercising a veto on all such legislation as may not be considered conducive to the general well-being of the Empire. The Ministry or Cabinet, together with the Head of the State, form the Executive Council, which consists of a Colonial Secretary, an Attorney-General, a Treasurer-General, a Commissioner of Crown Lands, and a Secretary for Native Affairs. All these Ministers have permanent Under-Secretarys.

The Legislature consists of two houses—*i.e.*, the House of Assembly, numbering 74 Members, and the Upper House, numbering 22 Members, who are entitled to be designated "Honourable."

The defence of the Colony is in the hands of permanent and volunteer forces—comprising Cavalry, Artillery and Infantry—in all about 3,223 men, who form the nucleus of an army of friendly natives, who are always available and form a fine fighting force.

The religious and educational advantages of the Colony are numerous and well cared for. The combined congregations, as far as can be learned, number 383,765, of which 232,046 are of European extraction and 150,719 coloured nations and tribes. The denominations are Dutch Reformed Church, Wesleyan. Church of England, Congregationalists, Independents and London Missionary Society, Moravians, Rhenish Mission, Roman Catholic, Free Church of Scotland, Baptists, Lutherans, French Reformed Church, Free Protestant and Hebrew and Mahommedans. There are many Christian Missions at work amongst the tribes, and good earnest work is being done, though the seed sown in these days will, very likely, not bear fruit until the next generation. Every encouragement is given to the natives to improve their condition, and much labour and capital spent yearly on the noble work.

Educationally speaking, the Cape Colony is something more than merely abreast of the times. Considering the difficulties and discouragements to be overcome in a new country, it is marvellous that so much real solid work has been and is being achieved. This happy result is to be traced to the unanimous way in which the Government works with the people.

The Governmental expenditure in this department ranges from £95,000 to £100,000 a year: of this amount the colleges, of which there are five in connection with the University of Good Hope, absorbed £8,000; the Public Schools, £28,000; the Mission Schools, £18,000; and the Aborigine Industrial Schools, £21,000.

The scenery of the Cape Colony is, in many parts, grand and romantic in the extreme. On the Sneeuwbergen range of mountains there is a spot known as the "Valley of Desolation." Here vast masses of rock have been tossed and torn by natural agencies into a thousand fantastic shapes.

Viewed under favourable circumstances, one could almost fancy the place a fit home for the mysterious creatures who exist only in the fervid imaginations of those romancers to whom reference has been made in an earlier stage of this volume. Amongst these tumbled and irregular masses of basaltic rocks herds of baboons dwell in undisturbed security. Some of these animals are almost as large as men, and, though not especially dangerous, are not such as one would elect to " meet by moonlight alone."

There is a case on record of a traveller who, encountering a gang of them, shot at and killed one of their number. Instantly the others showed fight, and, but for his presence of mind, would have played havoc with him. Seeing the hopelessness of coping with such numbers, he instantly fell to the ground, and lay there shamming death. The creatures, after handling him roughly for a few moments, passed on, and left him to his own devices, which may be summed up in instant and inglorious flight.

Deer of various kinds are to be had, but this question will be dealt with when, in the course of our journey, we win our way to the wilds and encamp in the untrodden places.

In order to exhaust the picturesque beauties of the Cape Colony, we should have to review the greater part of the country, for there are—excepting on the great plains—but few districts without especial scenic charms. The tourist will find himself literally bewildered by rival claims of beauty, which, after all, is a matter of taste, both humanly and geographically speaking, for that which charms one, will not affect another. In penning such a volume as the present, unless a full and consecutive survey be given, it is perhaps as well to abstain, and allow the traveller to select for himself the spot best calculated to meet his views and purposes.

CHAPTER III.

PHYSICAL GEOGRAPHY, GEOLOGY AND MINERALS OF THE CAPE COLONY.

THE physical geography of the Cape Colony, and indeed of all South and South-east Africa, can be best described as consisting of a series of steppes springing from the sea coast, and gradually rising to an altitude of about seven thousand feet, where large, open, and almost treeless plains, form the principal features. Table Mountain we have already described. The Winterhoek (6,840 ft.) forms one of another range further inland, where it forms the chief watershed of the west. The vine-growing valleys of Stellenbosch, Paarl, Drakenstein, Wellington, &c., are located on the seaward slopes of an irregular chain of mountains, that extend from Cape Hangklip, near False Bay, northwards through Namaqualand to the Orange River. The next, or Zwartberg range, which may be classed as third in the series, encloses on one side Gahamaland Karoo, Tradouw, and the district of Ladysmith, while on the other it bounds the "Great Karoo." The same range extends eastward, and attains an altitude of about 6,000 ft. The Great Karoo is not, properly speaking, a desert, except in exceptionally dry seasons, when the herbage becomes parched and dry. Behind this region there rises a ridge of table-topped hills, known on the western side as the Roggeveld and Nieuwveld Mountains, and on the eastern as the Sneuwbergen. From the central range of the latter mountain, an arm turns off to the eastward, where it is known as Tandtjesberg, Zwagershoek and Boschberg. These form a junction with the Great Winterberg Mountains (7,000 ft. in height), and thence sweeping on along the heights of the Katberg, Elandsberg, Giakaskop, the Hogsback and the Amatolas, terminates in the Buffalo and Kologha ranges in King William's Town division. This grassy and open plateau stretches still further northward, where it rises by another steppe to the Stormberg Mountains in the districts of Wodehouse, Aliwal North and Barkly. It then joins the Drakensberg Mountains which attain an altitude of 10,000 feet above the sea. These will be described in succeeding chapters.

The geology of these mountains has been the subject of much study by those who have spent time amongst them, and their nature is fairly well known. Briefly, we may sum them up as being, on the mountains nearest the seaboard, of palæozoic or primary formation, pierced in places by intrusive rocks. Clay slate, sometimes broken through and altered by granite, forms the underlying nature of the whole of the southern districts.

From the Oliphant's River, northwards as far as Bushmansland, the prevailing formation is granite and gneiss, and it is in this region that the rich and valuable Namaqualand copper mines are situated. On the east side of the Colony, at George and Knysna, metamorphic rocks occur. Here also are quartz reefs, and there is great hope of a payable and valuable gold field being developed. While at Cape Town, in 1888, I learned that over 600 oz. of alluvial gold had been washed and banked, and that, as the works progressed, better and richer indications of gold were met with. But, at the same time, great caution must be observed by the inexperienced traveller or gold hunter in casting his lines in the region. No really extensive finds have yet been made—as far as my knowledge goes—and careful inquiries, prior to an investment of either capital or time, cannot be too strongly urged. At the foot of the Zwartberg range, which is regarded as of the Old Red Sandstone period, there is a limestone formation, which is said to belong to the Namaqualand schists formation. Here are situated the famous Cango Caves, which have been described, by those hardy mortals who have visited them, as of almost supernatural beauty. One may walk for long distances under crystalline arches, or beside snow-white stalactital columns, some of which are 70 feet in height and nine in girth. In the torchlight, they glitter and sparkle as though strewn with diamonds. The first cavern measures 600 feet in length, 100 in breadth, and 75 or 80 in height. The second, which is a veritable fairy chamber, is slightly smaller but infinitely more beautiful, its walls being draped by airy-looking imitations of lace, caused by the filtration of lime through the rocks. As yet, these caverns are but partially explored, but when they are thoroughly known it is commonly believed that they will rival the world-famed caverns of Elephanta in India.

The copper mines of Namaqualand have already been mentioned. It is written that, as early as 1685, the existence of this mineral was known, but that want of fuel and suitable appliances deterred the settlers from working the mines. These objections do not apply now, and though the industry is as yet but feebly attended to, we learn that 20,213 tons of ore, or thereabouts, annually leave the colony. The mines find work for about 2,500 persons. Another important item in this connection is coal. Seeing that vast woodless regions occur here and there in the Colony, the fuel supply is one of vital interest. In the districts of Albert, Aliwal, Wodehouse, Xalangar, and Maclear, vast deposits occur. At Molteno and Indwe the seams have been worked for years, and the construction of railways to the vicinity of the mines is rapidly bringing this necessary article within the reach of commerce.

CHAPTER IV.

GRIQUALAND WEST AND THE DIAMOND FIELDS.

THE history of Griqualand West forms a story of especial interest to both the statesman and the traveller. In 1854, the region belonged to the British Orange River Sovereignty. It was partially occupied by a Griqua chief named Waterboer. When the Sovereignty became an independent Dutch Republic, discontent was evinced by the natives, who fretted under Dutch rule. At first, no attention was paid to their protests, and seeing that the region occupied by them was an open, bleak and inhospitable one, it is not to be wondered at that the British Government paid scant heed to their complaints. But, when a traveller named O'Reilly, in 1867, found on a Dutchman's table amongst a lot of "pretty stones," a 21¼-carat diamond, worth £500, affairs assumed a more serious aspect. As a matter of fact, the weak Government of the Orange Free State was not in a position to control anything like a heavy digging community. Complications arose between the miners and land owners, and riots and bloodshed of a serious nature were imminent when the British Government stepped in and set the matter at rest, by annexing the region to the Cape Colony. This, as the event proved, was a wise and statesmanlike policy; for assuredly, had the region been allowed to continue much longer as a sort of no-man's-land, trade and commerce would have

KIMBERLEY. Mine and Town.
(From a Photograph by Robert Harris.)

suffered, and the prosperity and development of the
have been retarded for an indefinite time. For two ye
little was discovered, though the fact was established that
the banks of the Vaal River were rich in precious stones.

In 1869, a Dutchman purchased a stone from a Griqua
native for £400 worth of goods, and immediately sold it for
£10,000; its value to-day is estimated at £25,000. This stone
was called the "Star of South Africa," and is at present, I
learn, amongst the jewels of the Countess of Dudley. The
fame of the "Star" sent a rush of diggers of all sorts and
conditions to the bleak plains of Griqualand, where terrible
hardships were endured, and tragedies enacted which have
found their way into the romances and literature of the
century. In the latter part of 1870 or the beginning of 1871,
the deposits were located between the Vaal and the Mooder
Rivers, and immediately a camp was formed. Men swarmed in
from all directions, the camp became a town, and eventually,
the town a city. The result is, as I stated in the opening
section, that jewels to the weight of *six tons* and of a value of
£39,000,000 have been produced. Kimberley to-day is as well
appointed a city as any in the world, and as one strolls
through its broad open streets it is hard to realise that, but
eighteen years ago, the spot was to all intents and purposes a
desert.

Geographically, Kimberley lies, as was stated while treating
of the Cape Colony system of railways, 647 miles from Cape
Town, and 484 miles from Port Elizabeth (Algoa Bay). Its
communication by rail with these two sea ports has considerably altered and improved the condition of the town and
region. All the luxuries that the heart of man can desire; all
the requirements of life, let it be in what sphere it may, are met
and supplied here. So much has been written and in such
various directions, that any detailed and lengthy description or
guide to the place is almost unnecessary. The town is
situated on an open wind-swept plain, and is as strictly
controlled as that of any old and long-established land.

There are four mines, viz., Kimberley, Dutoitspan, De Beer's and Bultfontein—the latter being proclaimed in 1882. At first the demand for claims, or plots of ground for mining purposes, was so great as to necessitate division and subdivision of the tiny patches measuring only a few feet in superficial area. Many diggers who had paid the customary license of 10s. per month for their then unproved lots, disposed of them, in a few weeks, for £100. The value went on increasing until, in about ten years, these 10s. plots attained a value of £10,000 to £15,000 each. The mines are now practically controlled by two large companies, and find employment for many thousands of miners, overseers, clerks, share brokers, store keepers, and perhaps a few rogues.

The diamondiferous soil or clay forms a most interesting geological study. About one hundred or one hundred and fifty feet below the surface, the body of the matter changes from a soft loamy earth of a yellowish colour—which crumbles speedily when exposed to the air—to a hard, slate-coloured mass. When this discovery was made, a panic seized the community: the news flashed over the world, and the wiseacres, who had been propounding lengthy theories on the instability of the deposits, nodded their heads sagaciously. The old reproach, that for years has been extant, of South Africa being simply a country of samples was revived, and a check administered to the industry, but not for long: the new stratum was soon proved to be the real matrix, the former having simply been altered by atmospheric agencies. Confidence being reestablished, the development was rapid and healthy.

The method of recovering the diamonds from their lurking-places is simple, being laid down somewhat on the line of "the survival of the fittest." The "blue clay" is first pulverised by atmospheric agencies, and then passed through rotary washing machines, where the lighter particles are washed away and the heavier remain. Statistics show that in the eighteen months ending December, 1884, the Kimberley mine produced 1,429,727 carats of diamonds; while Bultfontein and Dutoitspan, each

The Union Steam Ship Company, Limited.

700,000; and in the following eighteen months De Beer produced 790,908 carats.

The province of Griqualand West is divided into three electoral parts, *i.e.*, Kimberley, Barkley West and Hay. Its area is about 17,000 square miles, the greater part of which is suitable for sheep farming.

CHAPTER V.

PONDOLAND AND THE PONDOS—ST. JOHN'S RIVER SCENERY—TRANSKEI.

WE must be grateful to the fates that govern the geographical distribution of the kingdoms and states of Africa. After wandering through the fertile and home-like regions of the Cape Colony, where trade and commerce, national activity and social progress, are in as active operation as in other and older lands, and after peeping at the busy toilers in the Diamond Mines, it is a grateful change to turn, for a space, to the comparative silence and restfulness of Griqualand East, Transkei, Tembu and Pondoland. Here we have a veritable dream realm of Arcadian beauty. Away in the westward, lifting their grand castellated cliffs 10,000 ft. into the sky, loom the Quathlamba or Drakensberg Mountains. From a very early period these solitudes have been regarded with superstitious awe by the natives. Circling round their crests, the lightnings flash and hiss, while the reverberating voice of the thunder wakes the "Spirit Voices" of the caverns, and calls into the air a thousand unaccountable sounds, at which the simple savages, whose minds are the reverse of scientific, cross their hands over their breasts and marvel.

The Union Steam Ship Company, Limited.

Amongst the time-worn cliffs, the wizards, those master minds of savage life, brewed their charms and uttered their incantations, while now and then the mysterious "white robe" of snow fell from "none knew whither."

The whole region from these mountains, right to the sea on the south-east coast, consists of a mingled mass of mountain, valley, forest and meadow. Flashing rivulets leap from rock to rock, tossing themselves over the chasms, or shining still and clear in the quiet pools.

The wonderful fertility and beauty of these districts, their warm balmy airs, and their beautiful semi-tropical foliage, are to be traced to the generous airs borne down on them by the trade winds of the Indian ocean, together with the strong current of heated water which pours through the Mozambique Channel, and along the coast. The two principal rivers in this vicinity are those of St. John's and Umtata. The former has especial claims on the interest of the English-speaking world, from the fact that a small but determined and brave community of Britons are endeavouring, and that with marked success, to establish a home and build up a colony there. In addition to this, the place is grandly beautiful, and well worthy the attention of the poet, statesman, tourist, traveller and colonist. I propose to deal in considerable detail with this section of our work, because, in the first place, the region has never, to my knowledge, been prominently brought before public notice, and in the second, it will serve as a pleasant interlude to the study of Natal and her history, where facts and figures of an extremely practical nature are dealt with.

A few years ago, the district which is now divided into Griqualand East, Tembuland, Transkei, and Pondoland, was ruled over by one independent and powerful nation called the Ama-Pondo. In extent it measures about 15,000 square miles, and possesses a sparse, migratory population of about half-a-million. Owing to tribal conflicts, the upper portion (Griqualand East) became almost depopulated, and was called "No-man's-land." Certain Griquas (a tribe of half-bred

Hottentots), emigrated to it from the Orange Free State, under a chief or captain named Adam Kok, who ruled them in a sort of way, until he died from injuries received by being run over by a waggon, in 1876. The district was then formed into an English Magistracy, in order to protect the remnant of the people; and I have it, on good authority, that this was one of the best managed territorial movements ever carried out by the English in Africa.

Tembuland and the Transkei, which are now provinces of the Cape Colony, with a white population of about 2,000, were occupied by sections of the Pondo tribe called Tembus. By their quarrelsome and improvident behaviour, they have so reduced themselves, as to be altogether unworthy of any consideration, so that the only part of the district which retains even a semblance of independence, is Pondoland. In the capacity of Special Correspondent for a daily newspaper, I have made several visits to this country, and on each occasion came away with higher hopes for the future of the place, as a field for European colonisation. The St. John's River, which flows through the centre of the country, is a broad, deep and navigable stream. The territory on its banks, which bears that name, was purchased some few years ago by the Cape Government from the paramount chief of Pondoland. Their purpose in doing so was, I am told, to secure the port and close it against the smugglers, who by supplying goods, such as liquor, gin and powder to the natives, were injuring their physique, and by arming them with deadly weapons raising up a danger for the future. St. John's River territory may be approached overland from the Cape Colony, *via* the Transkei and Tembuland; but in order to enjoy the full beauty of the scenery one must enter it from the sea, where the first objects to greet the eye are the romantic-looking "Gates of the River," as the two huge mountains that watch over the plains are called. Towering up in abrupt reaches to an altitude of 1,800 or 2,000 feet above the sea, they strike the visitor with a feeling of the keenest pleasure. Round their lower reaches are a number of low grassy hummocks, from behind which long stretches of dark forest extend inland until the many-coloured cliffs burst through them, and towering on to still higher altitudes, stand clear-cut and vivid against the sky.

On either side of the "Gates" the coast continues to give promise of picturesque beauty and fertility. About a mile to the southward of the river, Cape Hermes juts into the sea, which is churned white against the masses of dark conglomerate rock that fringe the coast. To the northward these rocks continue, while, just behind them, the rounded and verdant slopes of "White's Hammock" and "Porpoise Point" promise something in the way of open grass land. The foliage, as seen from the deck of a steamer, gives but a poor idea of the wealth of palm and fern to be seen ashore. But few signs of civilisation are visible, and those few of a primitive and homely nature.

As usual, there is a sand bar at the mouth of the river, but, as it carries a fair depth of water, it forms but a slight obstacle to entry. Once across this, the full glory of Nature—pure, simple, and unadorned—greets us. On the occasion of my last visit, the rising sun was just tinging the east, when the brave little exploring vessel (the *Lady Wood*) forced her way through the surf and swept into the broad and still lagoon. Under guiding signals from the shore, we steamed up stream for about a mile, and brought up at the "Needles," a pile of crystalline rock, upon which a tiny little galvanised nest of a custom-house has been built, a temporary wharf of bush poles had been constructed, and upon it we very gladly sprang. While the men whom I had brought with me were landing the expeditionary stores and setting up the tents, I walked off with one or two of the settlers to view the village, which is situate at the foot of one of the "Gates," or towering mountains. The settlement consists of about fifty neat little unpretentious cottages, a church, a jail, and a fort. The settlers, who muster about

100, were all pictures of health, while the ground seemed to be fertile and well watered. Behind the custom-house and across a clearing, were a couple of hotels, while several unfinished buildings close to them told of lively enterprise and hope. After making the acquaintance of such settlers as happened to be about, I returned to my camp and rested for an hour. Then setting out in a southerly direction, towards Cape Hermes, I passed the stockaded fort, which was garrisoned by a company of Cape Infantry, at that time under the command of Capt. Sprigg (a brother of Sir Gordon Sprigg). Holding my way still further, I soon surmounted the heights of the Cape, and turned to note the wild and beautiful prospect. By this time the sun had crept round to the west, and was flooding the distance with that rich yellow flare, which adds breadth and softness even to a commonplace scene. But there was nothing commonplace here. Like a map, spread out before me, lay the upper and the lower "Gates," for on a closer study of the formation of the hills, they must be so divided. On the right-hand side could be seen a vast natural tower of rock standing alone, as though built by Titan hands. The cavity between it and the mountain mass, further eastward, is called the "Devil's Bite." Nearer still, almost beneath me, the breakers from the bar dashed themselves against Porpoise Point, or went rolling in on the tawny sand, while their deep roar came up to me now and again softly and musically. Away in the extreme distance, delicately rounded hills swept into the haze, where the herds of game lay at rest, or the broad-winged eagles sailed slowly in mid air with never a sound to startle them, save the rippling of the brooks or the wind through the trees.

Next evening, having engaged boats, I embarked with the four trusty natives, who had shared my travels for years, and who had become endeared to me by many a perilous journey and hard campaign. Heading up stream, we soon found ourselves floating on a liquid mirror. The mountains on either hand come close up to the edge of the water, and in some places the thick tangled masses of foliage overhung the banks and formed Venetian arcades. As the sun set the wind fell, and the glassy water, taking the tints of evening, reflected the mountains and sky with such fidelity as to render it difficult to tell substance from shadow. At the first bend of the river, and right in the centre of it, is situated a low black rock, which is sacred to the name of "Jefferies." It appears that this worthy, who was a "sea cow" (hippopotamus) hunter, had heard that a fine specimen of that species of game was in the habit of taking its nightly rest here, so swimming off with his rifle, he lay in wait one night for the arrival of his prey. Before very long the monster came swimming down stream; scarcely had it set foot on the rock than Jefferies opened fire, and a long and tough battle was the result; at length, in his haste to reload, the hunter dropped his powder-horn into the stream, and victory, of course, was declared on the side of the "sea cow." Jefferies took to the water, intending to swim ashore, but the enraged creature overtook him, and one crush of its mammoth jaws ended the matter.

Passing on, we swept round a little cape, and found ourselves in what appeared to be a broad open lake. By this time the starlight was glancing on the river, affording just enough light to reveal the triangular fins of several prowling sharks, who, doubtless attracted by the paddle song of my men, were following us. Before very long the moon rose, and shed a light almost as bright as day over the wild and lonely scene.

On the left-hand side of the river, which, by the way, is called by the natives Umzimvuba (Place of Hippopotami), towers the western "Gates," in a sheer cliff of about 2,000 feet altitude. The sukerbosch trees that fringe the summit could be seen faintly outlined against the sky, while now and again a suspicious rustling in the forest near at hand, gave us timely warning of the presence of some of the prowling leopards for which the spot is celebrated. It was from the heights above mentioned that the ancient Kings—and the present chief of Pondoland, for the matter of that—cast those accused of practising magic to the disadvantage of their neighbours; many a score of unhappy wretches have been hurried out of life here, as the crushed skulls and fractured bones found, now and again, at the foot of the cliff testify.

On the right hand, towering high into the air, loomed the eastern "Gate," called by the natives "Echoban." This forms a portion of the tower mentioned a short time ago, in connection with the "Devil's Bite." Whether his satanic majesty ever really stayed for refreshment here, is not a question of especial interest to us just now, but the idea of its being demon-possessed seemed to me not at all an unlikely one, when, as our boat swept under its shadow, the silence was suddenly broken by the harsh yells and deep booming barks of a herd of baboons, whose slumbers had been disturbed by our advent. As they seemed reluctant to retire, I pulled a trigger on one, and managed to bring him down, whereupon the others redoubled their uproar and retired. Landing, we secured our prize, which was of large size, measuring nearly five feet from toe to crown. As the night was becoming clouded, and I wished to see the country clearly, camp was pitched here, and a tranquil rest obtained, for the indignation of our friends, "The Children of Toasi," as the natives poetically call the baboons, soon subsided.

Next morning, at earliest dawn, we moved on again. After about three miles, the river narrowed slightly, and the hills toned down from their wild grandeur to something more promising in the agricultural line. At this part, *i.e.*, about eight miles from the sea, is situated Banana Point, or Cape Difficulty, called by the latter name because of the baffling winds which swirl round it, rendering progress by sailing boat almost impossible. Calling a halt here, I pitched camp for a day or two, in order to explore the vicinity.

The foliage of this promontory is composed almost entirely

of wild banana (*Stailitzia Africanus*), mimosa and waterboom trees. In the reeds by the river edge, the weaver birds have built their nests by the thousand, and keep up a constant chattering that is not at all disagreeable. On the other side of the stream, the bank rises into a picturesque and interesting cliff of white quartz, which may prove to be gold bearing, but I had not the means of testing it with me.

At this point a tiny stream, clear and limpid as crystal, joins the main river; following on foot the course of this tributary, in a south-westerly direction, I chanced upon one of the sweetest glades imaginable. Giant trees stood about it on every side, their limbs interwoven and bound together by trailing creepers, from which flashed a veritable glory of azure, violet and white convolvulus flowers. The earth was strewn with large irregular masses of rock, over which soft moss had spread; while bracken, maiden-hair, and other varieties of ferns, formed thickets shoulder-high, through which I had to force my way. Being thirsty, I stooped by the brook to drink, but recoiled in disgust on tasting the water, which proved to be highly charged with sulphate of soda and salt. I afterwards learned, on inquiry amongst the natives, that the river is looked upon as a great "medicine place," and that by bathing in it, scurvy, ulcers, and wounds may be quickly healed, while rheumatic pains and lumbago are invariably cured after repeated ablutions. The only drawback to one's full enjoyment of the spot is the knowledge that leopards, and other gentry of that ilk, are equally fond of its quiet seclusion; and that while wandering and dreaming through the grateful and dimly-lighted arcades of the forest, the eyes of more than one of these tawny and treacherous felines are probably following and noting every movement. Another drawback is to be found in the presence of good old St. Patrick's pet aversion, *i.e.*, snakes: black and green mambas, of sizes ranging from two to ten feet, gracefully removed themselves in a most complaisant manner from my path, while tiny lizards, with flame-coloured heads, scuttled about in all directions.

I noticed some remarkably large scorpions about; one in particular, which I killed, measured four inches, and showed any amount of fight. I do not know whether it is usual for these reptiles to make any noise when enraged, but this one gave utterance to a very distinct and clearly-defined hissing and grating sound.

One might travel for weeks in this vicinity, and then leave half its beauties unexplored. Night overtook me before I struck the main river again, so I had, perforce, to bivouac in the forest. Next morning, I rejoined the men, and embarking, we pushed on for another five miles, when Mr. White's settlement was gained. This enterprising colonist is doing a good work in Pondoland, and by all accounts has firmly established himself in the good graces of the natives.

The river, at this point, separates into two channels, forming thereby an island of about ten acres in extent; here, also, the weaver birds have settled in vast flocks. These busy and intelligent little creatures are of a bright chrome-yellow colour, and are about the size of the English martin; they live on grain principally, and build most wonderful nests, which they roof in, and then by way of finish, add a long pendant tube, up which they have to climb in order to enter. The natives call them "amahlogohlgo," *i.e.*, the chatterers, and whenever a couple of women fall out and begin to recite poetry—or something else—at each other, they are invariably likened to "our feathered friends." The description is so fitting and comical, that, as a rule, the "row" is brought to a hasty close, and the *usual laughter and good humour* is restored.

Leaving the river at this stage we struck inland for a few days shooting, and while engaged in wearily wading through the long grass and tangled woods, had several interesting encounters with the wild denizens of the land. The country continues as fertile and as grand as ever, all it lacks being men to cultivate it, for it is but sparsely populated. In some of the native gardens I saw maize stalks measuring ten feet in height, while the cobs or heads of corn were large in proportion.

It was while shooting in this vicinity, that the sound of our firearms reached the royal ears of Umquekela, the king of Pondoland, and a couple of couriers came down to warn us to prepare for a royal visit next day. After regaling the messengers on venison, which was all I had, they returned, and next day, sure enough, the king appeared. He was a thin, blear-eyed looking creature, whose wasted limbs were swathed in the ample folds of an old overcoat. Mounted on a pony of Gothic and sombre aspect, " His Majesty," followed by a score of footmen bearing rifles and spears, approached the tent and dismounting seated himself on a convenient stone. After the first greetings were exchanged a deep and dismal silence fell on us. I knew that his mind was in the act of evolving the best and surest way of raising a gift. Presently his mouth-piece, a jovial looking and wily barbarian, shattered the silence by saying, " Yebo! white one, we all welcome you; the king delights in Englishmen and his territory is ever open to them." " The king is wise," was my answer. Whereupon silence crept over us once more, but the thirsty soul of the anointed one (for Umquekela loved gin) could not brook any further diplomatic or stealthy advances; he came right to the point. " See, white one," said he; "I come to bid you welcome. You walk over my hills, you drink and lave in my streams, you sleep in the shelter of my forests, you kill and eat my game; yet never a gift or a payment worthy of mention do you make. Let us be friends." "And am I not the king's friend?" I enquired; " Have I come here as an enemy; if so, where are my warriors?" " Let your words be fulfilled in a gift. In your native land, the rivers are of gin —so I hear—and blankets are stripped from the trees like bark; you partake of my rivers and trees, let me share yours also." Knowing how useless any attempt to disabuse his mind of this idea would be, I simply replied that " My native land was distant, I could not carry its rivers in my pocket, and further, that my blankets were all done." Once more a silence fell on us, and for a space the king sat wrapt in sorrow and overwhelmed with despondency.

Heaving a long and deep sigh he rose at length and remounting his steed rode away without saying farewell. Some months afterwards the poor old fellow died of excessive drinking, having first, however, lost the respect of his nation, which numbers 90,000. The country is at present ruled over by Sigeau, his heir, and is in a fair way to become a prosperous and happy state, under the British flag.

About a week after this I moved to another part of the country, and pitched my camp on a wooded plain close to the river. On the first night of our arrival in the new camp, while engaged in developing some photographic negatives which I had taken of the scenery, I heard a rustling in the reed-brake at the back of the tent. Thinking that it might be a jackal in search of a stray dainty, such as one of my jack boots, I crept round and hurled a geological specimen, weighing about a pound, at the spot. To my surprise, a large leopard sprang away with a rasping snarl, and vanished in the woods. The creature had, in its curiosity, actually crept to within twelve feet of my seat at the tent door. Next day we indulged in a grand and successful leopard hunt.

I may say here, that the Pondo tribe or nation is a docile and peaceable one; they are good labourers and faithful followers, though not as honest as the Zulus, or daring as the Swazies, whose acquaintance we will make when the course of our travels brings us to their country. As I have stated, the nation numbers, as nearly as I could gather, 90,000. They are polygamists, and barter their women, like other African nations. Their language is kindred to that of the Zulus, and like it, is most expressive and musical. Their ideas of a future state are hazy and undefined. A pumpkin or a goat, enjoyed in the present, in a Pondo's opinion, range high above all the future happiness which the missionaries are so earnestly expounding. They are, in fact, a practical and material-

The Union Steam Ship Company, Limited.

minded race. Their great luxury is tobacco, which grows in the land most luxuriantly, and there attains, in my opinion, a better flavour than in either Natal or the Transvaal. The territory of St. John's is normally only a small strip, measuring about ten miles by two or three miles along the river bank. Small land-grants are given to intending settlers by the Resident or Administrator, who is appointed by the Cape Government. The law of the country is Roman-Dutch, like that of the parent colony, while the natives are carefully handled and kindly treated.

The tourist will find in this vicinity an ample and little-known field for his energies and mettle, which must be of the best; while the sportsman may, in the forests, plains, and rivers, revel in almost every department of the hunt. Roads have been constructed right through the country. Hotel accommodation is very scarce; but to make up for these disadvantages, he will find that a rough and ready hospitality is the rule of the land.

CHAPTER VI.

A Sketch of the Early History of Natal.

THE Port of Natal was a Christmas gift to the world, for, as I have already shown, it was discovered by Vasco de Gama on that holy festival day, in the year 1497. Like all other Christmas gifts, it is delightful. With a climate similar to that of Pondoland, which we dealt with in the last section, it possesses all the comforts of civilisation and the charms of a well-bred society.

Before proceeding to review its features and institutions, perhaps it may be well to glance briefly at its past history, for I have noticed that when our knowledge of a person or place is superficial, our interest is apt to be fleeting.

As an Imperial dependency which is daily rising to higher levels of usefulness and distinction, Natal is well worthy of most serious attention at the hands of all classes of readers, whether they be intending emigrants, tourists, sportsmen, gold hunters, or stay-at-home folk. After the eventful Christmas morning, nearly four hundred years ago, the country lay untouched and unexplored, except by some English sailors who, in 1683, were cast away near Delagoa Bay, which is about 325 miles to the north of Durban, and eleven hundred odd from the Cape of Good Hope, for the Port of Natal is 810 miles north of that place. These men, in their wonderful walk, saw much of the country, and on their arrival at the

Cape trading settlement, made a most favourable report on it. Three years later, in the same century, the *Stevenisse*, a Dutch ship, was wrecked on the coast ; and the sailors, after building a boat for themselves from the wreckage, sailed to the Cape, where another favourable report was made, which resulted in a slight exploration of the region. In 1721 an attempt by the Dutch to found a trading station there failed. We next hear of the slave-traders availing themselves of the commodious harbour and teeming native population.

It appears that considerable physical alterations have taken place in the port since these early times ; for instance, the Umgeni River, which now enters the sea four miles further to the northward, was said to flow into the head of the bay, and that the present " Bluff" was in fact an island, with a narrow channel between it and the mainland, at or near Isipingo. Whether this be so or not is a matter of small moment, for the present state of affairs is very satisfactory. From published reports of that period we learn that the " country was teeming with cows, calves, oxen, steers and goats ; while in the woods, elephants, rhinoceros, lions, tigers, leopards, eland and other deer, as well as buffalo, hippopotami, wild hogs, wolves, hyænas, and hosts of smaller creatures, such as a species of civet, wild cats, otters and ant-bears abounded.

About seventy years after these reports were made—that is to say, about the year 1800—we learn that the native tribes in this region were numerous and powerful ; while further north, "a few days' march," a mighty nation, named the Amazulu, were daily rising into power by conquests achieved under their brilliant emperor Chaka.

Before long, the attention of this warrior was turned to the region now known as the Colony of Natal, and with one fell swoop he cleared it of cattle, and left behind him desolation, death and misery. The few survivors of the shattered tribes led lives of misery in the woods, while the marauding parties of the victorious Zulus moved about destroying gardens, burning villages, and generally playing havoc with

the country. Three years after this invasion (1823-4), some
English settlers made their appearance: Leuts, Farewell and
King, together with others of lesser note—such as Isaacs,
Thompson and H. Fynn—arrived. These succeeded in collecting the lurking and cowed natives round them, and each
became the head or chief of a clan, which in time formed
a protection and safety to the land. Meanwhile Chaka, the
conquering hero, was assassinated by a relative named
Dingaan, who reigned in his stead. About this time, a sort
of contract was entered into between the Zulu king and the
Whites, by which the right to settle in and about the Port
of Natal was accorded them. Had they worked well together
all might have been well, for their combined forces formed
a powerful barrier to native invasion, but jealousies broke out
amongst them, for each wanted to be "Inkosi Inkulu" (great
chief). Before long, the wily enemy saw the joint in their
armour, and availed himself of it to obtain especial and secret
gifts from each. No doubt he hugged himself with delight
whenever each new aspirant approached—for a word in his
ear meant a valuable and useful gift in his hand. It was at
this most opportune time (1838) that another band of white
settlers appeared on the scene in the persons of the Dutch
"Voor trekkers," who left the Cape Colony in indignant
protest against the British policy there, as will be remembered.
Their chagrin, on finding that the English were in the
field before them, may be imagined. During the months
intervening between their departure from the Cape and their
passage up the Drakensberg into Natal, much that is stirring
and romantic happened to them. Referring to the very meagre
records of the time, we learn that under leaders, named Trichard,
Gert Maritz, Uys, Landtman, Rudolph, and Retief, the emigrants, numbering in all about 7,000, formed themselves
into caravans, which stretched, in some cases, for miles upon
miles across the country. Taking a course through the
region now known as the Orange Free State, in order to
avoid certain hostile tribes, they held their way parallel

with, and on the western slopes of, the Drakensberg Mountains, until in the neighbourhood of the Vaal River. Here the valiant "trekkers" met with the powerful and warlike Matabele tribe, and in the resulting battle twenty-eight of their champions fell, while the barbarians captured several herds of cattle and carried off some of their children. This check was followed by another, in which twenty-five men and women fell, while their property became the spoil of the enemy. A few of this second party escaped, however, and fled back to warn several succeeding caravans. These drew themselves together in time to meet (on the 29th of October, 1836) the combined army of the Matabele. Forming "Lagaars" or stockades of their waggons, and being armed with "roers" (elephant guns), they held their own against their agile and dauntless assailants. In the battle, as far as I can learn, only two "Boers" (farmers) were killed and twelve wounded, while a heavy loss was inflicted on the savages, who retired discomfited and defeated.

Passing on, after having carried the war into the country of Moselekatze, the Matabele chief, as shown elsewhere, the emigrants turned eastward, and approached the Drakensberg Mountains for the purpose of reaching the coast. But an enemy set fire to the great prairies between them and the mountain range, thereby not only endangering their lives, but preventing their advance—for the hills, after the passage of the flames, were left without a blade of grass for the cattle to eat. Under these circumstances, a large camp was made, where the main body remained, while Retief and about seventy men rode on to spy out the land (what a wonderful analogy there is, by the way, between this event in modern history and the Israelitish record of the escaped bondsmen of Egypt, as set forth in the Scriptures). From the summit of the Drakensberg, the pioneers had a grand view of "the promised land." Since then I have time and again revelled in the same fair scene. It is difficult, in prosaic words, to convey any true or vivid description of this divinely grand prospect. The man who can stand on those rugged and majestic mountains, and look across the vast fertile and unspeakably beautiful region without a thrill of the most exquisite delight, must be dead indeed to all that is inspiring and good in Nature. The same scene is to be enjoyed to-day, and I venture to say, without hesitation, that one day spent in these elevated latitudes is worthy *a journey across the world.*

Even these rugged and practical farmers, fresh as they were from the turmoil of battles and the more terrible toils of moving waggons through the roadless and undefined wilderness, were overcome with awe and delight, 20,000 miles of Eden-like meadows, hills, valleys, rivers and forest lay there, as they fondly hoped, awaiting them. Passing on, Retief and his brave little band descended the Berg, and traversing the country approached the encampment or village of the dreaded Emperor Dingaan. This crafty and brutal assassin received them with apparent friendliness, and after hearing their request for permission to settle in the land which was his only in name, most graciously granted them their wish. After the business of the meeting was over, he expressed a wish to entertain them with a grand review of his army. Delighted with his urbanity they agreed to wait the assembly of the warriors. For two days the army, numbering over 4,000 stalwart savages, paraded and went through their warlike exercises. This over, Dingaan, having impressed the Boers with a sense of his might, requested them, in order, as he said, to prove the sincerity of their devotion, to go up and chastise a certain freebooting Mantatee chief, named Sikonzella. "What can I do?" wrote Retief to his friends in camp, "otherwise than trust to the Almighty, and patiently await His will." Fortune, however, favoured the Bellerophon-like enterprise of the pioneers, for they compelled the Mantatee chief to obedience.

After this, Retief returned to the main camp of the emigrants, who by this time had crossed the Drakensberg and entered the region now known as Blawkrantz and Weenen, in Natal. Taking about 200 of the very pick of the caravans, he set out once more to greet the king. An immense concourse received them at the royal palace. Dingaan expressed himself as pleased with their success, and feasted them right royally. As a further proof of his good will, he granted them the country between the Tugela and St. John's River, utterly regardless of the fact that already he had handed it over to the British settlers, who were meanwhile peacefully labouring at Port Natal. This business being thus, as the Boers thought, satisfactorily arranged, festivities were indulged in, and great good feeling expressed on both sides. Still, from force of old habit, the Boers retained their rifles in their hands always. Dingaan, noticing this, made a special request that they should lay them aside, in order to enter into a conference with him. Incautiously, the pioneers complied, and instantly were seized and dragged to the place of execution, where they were foully murdered.

The war cry now spread, and the savage hordes poured themselves against the devoted Dutch and English settlers. After several victories and one or two drawn battles, Dingaan was defeated, and murdered by one of his own captains named Umpanda. This chief was proclaimed King of the Zulus by the Boers, who, at the same time, formed themselves into a Government, which was called the Republic of Natalia. It was in these struggles that the grim determination of the Rhinelanders showed itself, and won for them such decisive victories. And it was in these struggles that South Africa added to her roll of heroes a goodly list of names whose representatives to-day do no discredit to the valour of their fathers. Now comes the saddest part of all the history; one may look on the feuds between barbarian and Christian men with a certain amount of philosophy, for it is natural to expect conflicts between such diverse natures, but when Christian men, fellow-settlers and brother pioneers, turn upon and rend each other, the case is different. Some of our historic heroes have to climb down from the pedestals of fame which their bravery and enterprise had raised them to, and others again must in charity to their descendants be put out of sight and mind. The English at the port, and the Dutch further inland, fell to blows over trifles, and a useless and bloody war was the result. Having done my best to set the hazier parts of the colonial history before my readers, I must refer them to other works for the melancholy record of the Anglo-Dutch Colonial War, which resulted in the fall of the Republic, and the establishment of the British Colony of Natal.

TOWN HALL, DURBAN, NATAL.
(*From a Photograph by Robert Harris.*)

CHAPTER VII.

NATAL OF TO-DAY.

ATAL has been, with justice, called the "Garden of South Africa." It lies, as a glance at the map will show, between Pondoland and Zululand, and has a superficial area of 21,150 square miles, or about thirteen and a-half million of acres. Its boundaries are British Zululand on the north; Pondoland and Griqualand East on the south; Basutoland, the Orange Free State and the Transvaal on the west; whilst it shows a seaboard of 180 miles on the east.

The view from the deck of the steamer as she lies at the outer anchorage is a pleasant and interesting one. On one hand the wooded heights of the "Bluff" clothed in dense forests, jut into the sea and trend away into the distance; on the other the Town is faintly hinted at by the appearance of a few spires and towers over the fringe of bush that skirts the shore. The distance is bounded by the Berea, with its villas and cottages, while in the foreground the masts of the shipping proclaim the commercial importance and life of the place.

Durban, the seaport of the Colony, may be divided into three parts: first, the Point and Addington, which is a town in itself; second, the main or business centre; and third, the Berea or residential part. The entrance to the harbour has been hitherto somewhat obstructed by a bar similar to that at the mouth of the St. John's River; but owing to the effectual and skilfully carried out harbour improvements, it is daily being removed, and already ships of one thousand tons and over may enter in safety and discharge alongside the wharves, where ten years ago vessels of four and five hundred tons could not venture with any degree of safety. Once over this long-standing and somewhat exaggerated danger, the voyager finds himself in a landlocked harbour measuring about four miles by three. It is enclosed on the south by a long wooded range, called the "Bluff," upon the extremity of which stands the lighthouse, and where even in these degenerate days of ultra-civilisation, good shooting is to be had.

Near the head-waters of the bay are a group of tiny islands where pic-nic parties most do congregate. Three rivers—named the Umbelo, Umhlatazan and Manzie-manyam (Blackwater)—flow into it from the west and north-west. Slightly further north, the Congella flats and mangrove thickets afford shelter to droves of sea-fowl; while on the southern edge, on a picturesque plain, stands the town itself. Landing from the steamer, the traveller will be pleasantly surprised at the bustle and progressiveness of the place. Broad, solid, and well-constructed wharves laid with rails, towering warehouses, steam cranes, railway engines screaming and puffing, and the eternal rumbling of wheels, greet his eyes and ears whichever way he looks. A ride—either by train, tram, or bus—of two miles, through a continuous mass of substantial structures, will take him through Addington and into Durban proper. Here again, the solidity and English appearance of the streets, and town generally, will serve to convince the most sceptical of the wealth, importance and value of the Colony as a field for enterprise and labour. The Town Hall, which has been erected at considerable cost, is a stately building, and forms a fitting centre-piece to the town. The streets are laid down at right-angles, and West Street (the principal thoroughfare) is broad, well built and lighted. Goods of all descriptions are to be had at a very slight advance on English cost. The population of Durban is estimated at 17,000, of which 4,385 are natives, 3,000 Indians, and the remainder whites—principally British.

The Union Steam Ship Company, Limited.

Pietermaritzburg — commonly called "Maritzburg"— the capital of the Colony, is situated about fifty-four miles by rail inland, and to the north-west of the port. It was founded by the early Dutch settlers, and is a comfortable, well-appointed and busy commercial centre. At first it does not strike one as being so thoroughly English as Durban, but that feeling soon passes off. The public buildings of the city are stately and handsome, while the streets are broad, and in many cases planted with shade trees. The whole population of Maritzburg is 15,767; slightly less than that of Durban. This number is made up as follows :—Whites 9,251, Indians 1,654, Natives 4,291, Hottentots and others 571. Amongst its public institutions I may mention a Swimming Club, Reading Room and Public Libraries, an Agricultural Society, Botanic, Benevolent, and Horticultural Societies; while Friendly Societies, such as Odd Fellows, Foresters, Freemasons, &c., are in great repute.

Maritzburg was connected by rail with Durban, in 1880. Of other townships there are great numbers. Chief amongst which I may mention, Howick, Weston, Estcourt, Colenso, Ladysmith, Newcastle, Pinetown, York, Nottingham, Stanger, Richmond, Greytown, Umzinto, Harding, New Hanover, Willowfontein, Marburg, Hermansburg, Verulam, Victoria Stanger, and Isipingo. The railway system of Natal is being rapidly extended, in order to meet the increased requirements of the Gold Fields trade. At present three lines start from Durban. One, called the South Coast line to Isipingo, a distance of ten or twelve miles; another, called the North Coast line, to Verulam, 25 miles; and the third or main line, to Ladysmith in the uplands of the Colony, 189 miles. The fares to Ladysmith are—1st Class, £2 7s. 3d., 2nd Class, £1 11s. 6d., 3rd Class, 15s. 9d., with allowance for luggage. These fares are of course subject to variation. The main line passes through Maritzburg, and by it some most interesting scenery can be enjoyed.

The Government of Natal is of a unique description, it

being neither a Crown Colony, nor an independent one. The Governor is appointed by the Crown, as are the heads of Departments, such as the Colonial Secretary, Attorney-General, Surveyor-General, Postmaster-General, Secretary for Native Affairs and Treasurer-General.

The Legislative Council is, with the exception of certain Government nominee members, elected by the colonists. All Bills passed by this body must first receive the Imperial sanction before they become law. The defence of the country rests, of course, under these circumstances, with the Crown, though hitherto the colonists have acquitted themselves bravely. A strong Volunteer force of over one thousand colonists is always ready to take the field, and as it is divided into cavalry, artillery, and infantry, it forms no mean factor in the Imperial estimation. The Government supports them in a most generous manner. In addition to this, the Natal Mounted Police is really a strong and well-drilled cavalry corps, numbering usually about 100, ready at a moment's notice to take the field.

The physical geography of the country is similar to that of the south-eastern parts of the Cape Colony; while, by reason of its position, its climate is, on the coast at any rate, of a semi-tropical nature. This arises from the same causes as stated when dealing with the climates of Pondoland and St. John's River territory. Commencing at the coast, the country rises in an almost regular series of steppes, which culminate in the Drakensberg range of mountains, with an altitude of 10,000 feet above the sea. Owing to this formation, it will be seen that a series of climates may be enjoyed, ranging from the moist warm coast lands to the broad open wind-swept and sometimes bleak levels, called "Up-country." These steppes may be enumerated as follows:—

The Coast level extends inland, roughly speaking, three miles. Then the Berea and its continuations, which attain about 400 feet of altitude. Then the Fields Hill and Noodsberg ranges, 1,000 feet. After these, we may estimate the

Inchanga at 2,000 feet. Passing it we strike the elevated plain south and east of Pietermaritzburg (3,500), and from them by a gradual rise to the Drakensberg, which forms the watershed of the country, and attains, as has been stated, an altitude in places of 10,000 feet. This is simply an approximation, but it will serve to illustrate the broad features of the place. For about thirty miles inland, sub-tropical and tropical agriculture prevails: tea, coffee, tobacco, sugar, arrowroot, ginger, bananas, pineapples, oranges, &c., grow luxuriantly. The district is well wooded and watered, free from fever, and healthy, though somewhat relaxing.

Inland of this belt is what may be called the Middle District. The air is cooler, and the productions almost identical with that of England; wheat, oats, barley, turnips, forage, potatoes, and all European cereals, thrive. The pasturage is good, and in the kloofs (valleys) wood in abundance is to be had. The climate here loses the coast heat in a great measure, is entirely healthy, and has an even temperature throughout the year. The farms closely resemble those in an English county, while society of a most enjoyable description is to be had. The upper district, which lies contiguous to the Berg, is suitable chiefly for grazing stock, though wheat, and other produce of a similar nature, thrives in the more sheltered valleys. Sheep, cattle, and horse farming are the chief features of the place, while in limestone and coal it is especially rich.

The population of Natal is estimated at 485,000, made up as follows: European, 45,000; Indian emigrants, 40,000; natives, 400,000. Of the Europeans, the bulk are colonial born. The Indians were introduced as labourers, because the natives, like all primitive men, have a decided aversion to hard work, on the plantations. The great mass of the population is, as the above figures show, made up of descendants of the original tribes who took refuge under the early settlers. In addition to the natural increase which has taken place, their numbers have been largely supplemented by refugees from the surrounding native states. They have districts, called "locations," set apart for them, the total extent of which exceeds 2,000,000 acres. Native chiefs are either appointed by our Government or elected by the natives. Being polygamists, they cannot come under our code of laws, so the Government, with a wisdom which, from my knowledge of the natives, I may venture to designate as questionable, have acknowledged their ancient codes, and, as a consequence, Natal has two or more sets of laws—one for the Black, one for the White—and one might almost say a third for the Indian, whose interests are so carefully and captiously attended to by the Indian Government as to require a special Court, which is presided over by an officer called "The Protector of Indian Emigrants." The bulk of the natives live at their ease in these locations, the land being free to them and exceedingly fertile, their wants being few, and taxes light (14s. per hut a year). They lead a life of lazy luxury, that does more to retard their intellectual and social progress than any amount of active depravity would effect. The rest of the land is distributed as follows: 8,000,000 acres acquired by grant or purchase by Europeans, while two and a-half millions remain in possession of the Crown, and, as yet, unappropriated.

The following extract of the law governing the sale and transfer of Crown lands will be read by intending purchasers with interest:—

RULES AND REGULATIONS FOR THE DISPOSAL OF THE CROWN LANDS IN THE COLONY OF NATAL.

I.—Sale of Crown Lands, exclusive of Crown Reserves, Township Lands and certain Pasture Lands.

1. Exclusive of all lands which are already, or which shall hereafter be, set apart for public purposes, either permanently, such as Crown forests and lands required for the purposes of public defence and convenience, or temporarily, such as lands required for the formation of "special settlements" under the provisions of Law No. 21, 1876, or otherwise for the time

A STREET IN DURBAN.
(From a photograph by the Author.)

being, such as certain pasture lands under the Drakensberg not adapted for agriculture, and certain coal-bearing lands in the Division of Newcastle, in the County of Klip River, as hereinafter shall be defined by public notice, and the conditions for renting out or leasing of which for grazing purposes are hereinafter separately dealt with, and exclusive also of township lands, as hereinafter named and described, and the conditions for the sale of which are herein also separately dealt with, the unappropriated waste lands of the Crown are open for sale, in lots varying from 10 to 2,000 acres.

2. All lands so opened for sale as aforesaid will be sold in freehold, and by public auction only, to the highest bidder, and the upset price of such lands shall be at the rate of 10s. per acre.

3. All lands will be sold subject to the following special servitudes which shall be set forth in the title-deeds, viz. :—

(a) All authorised roads, railways, telegraphs, thoroughfares and watercourses, now made or running on the said lands, shall remain free and uninterrupted, as in their present or past use.

(b) The said lands shall be liable, without compensation to any proprietor, or to any sub-grantee or lessee thereof, to have any roads, railways, railway stations, telegraphs or watercourses made over any part of them for the public use and benefit by order of the Colonial Government, except those parts in which any building may actually be thereon erected at the time when any such roads, railways, railway stations, telegraphs or watercourses may be required to be made, in respect of which building, if required to be removed for any such purpose, reasonable compensation shall be made by the said Government.

(c) The said lands shall be liable, without compensation to any proprietor, or to any sub-grantee or lessee thereof, to the entry thereon by any person, by order of the Colonial Government, to remove therefrom any coal or any other mineral that may be found thereon, and also to the right of the Colonial Government to carry out such workings on or in the said lands as may be required for the removal or utilisation of such coals or other minerals, and also reserving to the Colonial Government the right of entry on said lands, and removing therefrom such materials, not including timber or wood, as may from time to time be required for the construction and repairs of any part of any public road running through the said lands.

(d) The said lands, if 500 acres or more in extent, will be sold subject to the general right of all travellers to outspan upon them, in suitable situations, for not more than 24 hours, unless longer detained by just cause, as provided for under Law No. 9, of 1870, and to such other regulations relative to outspan as may hereafter be deemed necessary, and declared by the Government for the interests of the public.

4. Persons desirous of acquiring Crown lands by purchase must make application in writing to the Surveyor-General, and must set forth in such application the division in which the land they wish to purchase is situated, and, as far as practicable, its position, boundaries, and extent. Should the Surveyor-General see no objection to the land so applied for being disposed of by public sale, he will submit the application for the approval of the Governor, and, upon such approval, he will call upon the applicant to deposit with him the probable amount of fees required for the inspection, survey, and erection of beacons, in accordance with the tariff of survey fees, as fixed under Government Notice No. 124, of the 28th October, 1861, or such other Government notice as may be at any time issued.

5. In the event of the sale of the lands applied for, the expenses attending the survey will be borne by the purchaser, and, should the original applicant not become the purchaser, the fees deposited by him for the survey will be returned to him, but, should no sale take place, no such refund will be made.

6. The Surveyor-General, on receiving the survey fees, will proceed with the inspection and survey of the lands for which application has been made, subject to the general conditions contained in Schedule B, and the applicant shall, personally, or by duly appointed deputy, attend at the inspection and marking off, by beacons, of the boundaries of the lands at the points where the lines intersect, and at such other points along the boundaries as may be necessary, and, upon the completion of such survey, notice shall be published by the Surveyor-General in the *Government Gazette*, at least one month before the day of sale, setting forth that the lands so surveyed will be offered for sale by public auction at a time and place named in the notice.

7. On the day named in the said notice the Surveyor-General shall cause the lands to be put up for sale by public auction.

8. The lands, having been put up to public auction, shall be sold to the highest bidder, who shall be deemed to be the purchaser, and who shall, on the day of sale, pay to the Surveyor-General, or person representing him, the expenses of the survey in full, and who shall, within three months from the day of sale, pay one-tenth part of the total purchase amount.

9. Upon the aforesaid payments being made, the Surveyor-General shall issue an occupation certificate to the purchaser, in the form hereunto annexed, and shall attach to the certificate a diagram showing the position, extent and boundaries of the land, together with a copy of the conditions of

such occupation, which condition shall commence to take effect from the date of the issue of the occupation certificate.

10. The condition of such occupation shall be as follows:—Within six months of the issue of the said occupation certificate, the purchaser to whom such certificate is issued shall enter upon beneficial occupation of the land. To constitute such beneficial occupation there must be continuous personal occupation by the purchaser, or by his agent, duly approved of by the Surveyor-General, during nine months in every year of the period for which the occupation certificate is issued, and the erection and maintenance of a suitable homestead or dwelling-house, and the cultivation, where the lands purchased are 100 acres or more in extent, of not less than one acre in every 100 acres.

11. Upon the issue of the occupation certificate, due notice of the purchase and of the certificate shall be communicated to the Resident Magistrate of the Division in which the land is situated; and at the close of the third year, commencing from the date of the issue of the certificate, and at the close of each succeeding year until the expiration of the tenth year from the date aforesaid, the holder of the certificate shall obtain from the Resident Magistrate of the Division a certificate showing that there has been such beneficial occupation.

12. At the close of every year, commencing from the date of the issue of the occupation certificate, the holder of the certificate shall also pay, either to the Surveyor-General or the Resident Magistrate of the Division, one-tenth part of the total purchase amount until the whole amount has been paid; and the Surveyor-General or the Resident Magistrate shall grant a receipt for each instalment so paid.

13. The Resident Magistrate shall forward to the Surveyor-General a duplicate copy of every certificate of beneficial occupation so given by him as aforesaid, and of every receipt for the instalments so paid, together with the amounts of all such instalments; and the Surveyor-General shall pay all moneys received by him, either from the occupant of the land or from the Resident Magistrate, into the Public Treasury, and shall keep an account of the same.

14. Upon receipt by the Surveyor-General of the final instalment of the purchase money, and upon receipt of the final certificate of beneficial occupation, and upon being satisfied that there has been such beneficial occupation, the Surveyor-General shall prepare a title vesting the land so occupied in freehold in the purchaser, which title shall be upon parchment, and shall be submitted to the Lieutenant-Governor for his signature and for the seal of the colony.

15. Upon the issue of every such title the Surveyor-General shall cause the same to be registered in the office of the Registrar of Deeds; and the

purchaser shall pay to Surveyor-General's office, in respect of such title and registration, a fee of forty shillings.

16. Portions of land, not exceeding 320 acres in the case of agricultural lands, and 1,000 acres in the case of pastoral lands, for the purchase of which in freehold special application is made to the Surveyor-General, and the sale of which is authorised by the Governor, shall be sold, in freehold, by public auction, to the highest bidder, at an upset price of £1 per acre.

17. The lands so sold as aforesaid shall be subject to the special servitudes set forth in Clause 3, and to no other servitude. The total amount of the purchase money must be paid by the purchaser of such lands within a period of three months from the day of sale.

18. In the case of *bonâ fide* immigrants from Europe, lands need not be sold by public auction. "Blocks" of land, not exceeding 50,000 acres in extent, may from time to time be surveyed and laid off as reserves for immigrants, to be disposed of under such conditions and regulations as the Governor in Council may from time to time direct to be issued.

19. For the purpose of these Regulations any portions of forest land of a greater area than 10 acres shall be deemed to be Crown forests. All such lands, and all lands upon which coal or other minerals are found, shall be permanently set aside and reserved to the Crown, and shall not be sold or alienated under these Regulations.

II.—*Sale of Township Lands.*

20. All township lands as set apart for sale in the townships hereinafter mentioned, and not reserved or otherwise appropriated, will be open, in lots not exceeding one erf, for sale to applicants, and for purchase at the several upset prices as below mentioned, and in the form and manner, and subject to the rules for times and mode of payment, as set forth above in the case of other Crown lands :—

	Upset price per erf.		
Colenso...	£25	0	0
Estcourt	25	0	0
Greytown	25	0	0
Glendale	3	10	0
Harding	10	0	0
Ladysmith	25	0	0
Newcastle	20	0	0
North Barrow...	12	10	0
Nottingham	25	0	0
Scottsburgh	12	10	0
South Barrow...	12	10	0
Stanger...	12	10	0
Weenen	25	0	0
Weston...	12	10	0

21. All town lots so sold shall be subject to the conditions of personal occupation by the purchaser, or by his agent, duly approved of by the Surveyor-General, or of useful occupation in the form of any building required for purposes of industrial business.

III.—*Rules applicable to all Lands sold under the above Regulations.*

22. In the event of any purchaser failing to fulfil the conditions of beneficial occupation, or occupation as hereinbefore mentioned in clauses 10 and 18, or failing to pay any annual instalment of the purchase price, the occupation certificate will be cancelled, all payments and improvements by the purchaser being forfeited, and the sale becoming null and void.

23. In the event of the decease or bankruptcy of the purchaser before the issue of the title to the land, his heirs, executors, administrators, or assigns, upon fulfilment of the conditions of occupation and payment of purchase price in the manner aforesaid, shall be entitled to all the rights of the original purchaser.

IV.—*Pastoral Leases and Licenses.*

24. The Crown lands lying under the Drakensberg, which are unsuitable for agriculture, and which will be hereafter described and defined by public notice in the *Government Gazette*, and those which are known as coal-bearing lands in the division of Newcastle, in the county of Klip River, will be open for occupation for grazing purposes, in areas varying from 500 to 5,000 acres, by annual license or by lease, for any term not exceeding ten years.

25. The upset rental of such lands will be at the rate of one penny sterling per acre per annum, and shall be payable every year in advance.

26. Any person desirous of renting or leasing any of the aforementioned lands must make application in writing to the Surveyor-General, setting forth the situation and extent of the land applied for; and every application so received will be registered, and a description thereof published in the *Government Gazette*.

27. Should there be no objection to the rental or lease of the lands so applied for, the Surveyor-General may, after one month from the date of the publication as aforesaid, issue at the upset rental the lease or license applied for; or, should he deem it advisable, offer the lease of the lands for which application has been made for purchase of the same by public auction.

28. Every lease will be subject to the servitudes attached to the land set forth in sections *a*, *b*, *c*, and *d*, of Regulation No. 3, and may be determined by either party upon twelve months' notice being given, the party giving such notice forfeiting the fees paid for survey, or it may be transferred

by the lessees, with the consent of the Surveyor-General, upon the payment of a transfer fee of ten shillings.

29. All licenses and leases so made shall be duly entered in a book to be kept for that purpose by the Surveyor-General; and every person to whom a license is issued shall pay to the Surveyor-General a fee of two pounds seven shillings, and every person to whom a lease is granted shall pay a fee of twenty shillings.

SCHEDULE A.

Occupation Certificate.

This is to certify that   , on the   day of   , in the year of Our Lord one thousand eight hundred and   , at public auction, of which notice was duly given in the *Government Gazette*, did become the purchaser of a piece of Crown lands situated in the county of   , being the lot known as   , bounded   , and containing   acres,   roods,   poles, be the same more or less, without any liability or claim for lesser or greater contents or acreage, as will more fully appear by the diagram framed by the Surveyor and hereunto annexed, with full power and authority to possess the same on certain conditions set forth at the sale, duly agreed to by the said purchaser, and repeated herein as following:—

SCHEDULE B.

General Instructions to be observed in the Survey of Crown Lands.

Each allotment shall be laid off with reference to natural boundaries and features, sharing equally with other lands left open as Crown lands, or surveyed at the same time for other applicants, arable, forest, and pasture capabilities.

2. Both banks of an important stream are not to be included in any one lot, unless the area of the lot is of such magnitude as to render such a condition necessary.

3. In surveying a river boundary, the bank of the stream or river is to be adopted as the boundary.

4. Lands let vacant, if of less width than one mile, must be included in the survey of adjoining lands; or the width must be not less than that of the land laid off or to be laid off, adjoining the same.

5. Each lot should be bounded by four approximately equal sides, deviations from this being only permitted with the view to connection with adjoining lands, or to taking advantage of river boundaries and other natural features referred to in paragraph 1. Such deviations, moreover, will be attended with a proportionate increase in the cost of the survey.

6. Each lot must be connected with the boundaries of some other lot of land which has been already laid off on the general plan in the Surveyor-General's office, and all details of such connection will be required with details of the survey of the lot so connected.

7. The proprietors of the adjoining lots of lands already laid off must be made aware by the Surveyor, through notice duly given, of any new survey or surveys to be undertaken. The beacons and boundary lines of such adjoining lots must be carefully compared, and the new survey will proceed from or be worked to them.

8. Before proceeding with any survey the details of all adjoining surveys must be taken by the Surveyor from the plans in the Surveyor-General's office.

9. The conditions laid down in Government Notice No. 32, 1862, with regard to the erection and delivery of beacons to intending purchasers, or to their deputies or agents, must be strictly observed.

10. Notice, within reasonable time, must be given by the Surveyor to each applicant or his agent, to enable him to be present at the survey, including the inspection; and to erect beacons, and take over the boundaries, according to the notice cited above.

11. In the event of several applications being made for land in a locality, the total area of which is not sufficient for the allotment to each applicant of the full area, the respective areas applied for may be reduced with the concurrence of the applicants; and if this is not practicable from any cause, natural and otherwise, the survey of each lot will take place in the order of the dates of the applications for the same.

12. Should any survey approach the boundary of the colony in the Drakensberg, it will be necessary to connect the same with that boundary line if the distance is less than one mile, and in no case may the space intervening between any survey and that boundary line be of less width than that of such survey.

Some of the productions of Natal have already been enumerated. The exports consist principally of wool, hides, skins, gold, ivory, and ore. The total value of imports, during the first nine months of 1887, was £1,653,841. Exports during the same period were valued at £741,948, but since then great advances have been made, owing to the increased activity and impetus given to commerce by the mineral development of the inland States. Of manufactures, but little can be said. Matches, jams, biscuits, and dried fruits are largely made for local consumption. Of waggon and carriage works, foundries and engineering establishments, there are several.

Touching the geology of the region. I have travelled over the whole of it, and, by putting my own observations beside those of others, have succeeded in collecting the following notes, which are correct as far as my knowledge goes. The granite base is visible only at the lowest parts of the river valleys, and on the coast hills. A line drawn due north from the Umtwalume River, in the southern extremity of the country, will touch all the parts of the country where granite and gneiss reach the surface through the covering of stratified rocks. Farther to the south this rock seems to form a distinct belt, which is lost for a time, but reappears in the lower parts of the Noodsberg Mountains in the north, and again, still further north, in the valley of the Tugela on the northern frontier of the colony, adjoining Zululand.

Mica schists, clay, chlorite and talcose slate are to be met with, where the granite base is exposed, nearly everywhere; they stand almost upright at an angle of from 65 to 75 degrees, with a pitch from north to south. They are particularly well seen in the Tugela valley. I have seen them also at the Umzimkuluwana and at the Um-pam-banyoni River (south). It is remarkable that the same pitch is to be noticed in the De Kaap and Tati fields. The Umzimkulu River, at about twelve miles from its mouth, breaks through crystalline limestone of enormous thickness. Messrs. Aiken Bros. have established marble and lime works here, which promise well. On both sides of the river, the marble forms precipitous walls of great height. This district covers about eleven miles. With respect to the mountain sandstones, and the general geology of the country, the following report, by an expert geologist, will, I think, be useful:—

"The sandstone plateaux, which are so characteristic of the African landscape, lie horizontally upon the old slate formation, and at some places on the granitic base. The sandstone, forming precipitous tablelands, has never been disturbed; nowhere is a folding of the deposits visible; only fractures run through the zone, in which masses of Aphanitic Diorite are seen, which have burst through the granite and slate formation; but nowhere is the sandstone raised up at an angle, or folded by the greenstone. The high plateaux are covered with a dense grass vegetation; the soil is extremely poor, and there is not even a shrub to interrupt the endless uniformity of the landscape. The rivers have made their way through the beds and strata of this sandstone,

Native Gold Fields, Tugela River.

thus forming precipices, at some points several thousand feet in height. The sandstone shows the same lithological peculiarities as the Table-Mountain Sandstone of the Cape, after which it is named. The tops of many of the 'table mountains' of the Colony are crowned by beds of dark basaltic greenstone, which contain fragments of quartz, granite and gneiss. In a variety of this igneous rock, from the 'Great Karoo,' I found traces of gold. I never found any organic remains in the sandstone of the Colony itself, except a thin soft shale, with much mica in it; which seems at the Krantzkop to be a bed in the sandstone, from which I got some small bivalves and a finely striated *Patella*, both too indistinct for determination. Such shale is also exposed near the upper drift of the Umkomazi river, near Richmond, and at several other places in the Colony. The Sluten-Kunga, Table Mountain near Pietermaritzburg, Inanda, and Noodsberg, are examples of the regular-shaped table mountains of South Africa. The same shales and quartz-sandstone from the Krantzkop, which drops nearly vertically down to the Tugela River, about 3,800 feet. The high plateau is capped with melaphyre-like greenstone. The basis of the Tugela valley is granite and is covered with the so-called 'Doorns' (Thorns), the celebrated mimosa vegetation of South Africa; the great mass of the mountain is built up of sandstone, and crowned with basaltic greenstone. In this locality, but on the Itemani side of the Krantzkop, I found the small traces of organic remains in the shaly bed of the sandstone which I mentioned above."

The Karoo Formation.—So called after the Karoos, the immense plains of the interior, as they are principally composed of strata of this formation, which has its greatest height above the sea in the Drakensberg range. The lower part of the land on the Natal side of this range rests partly upon the Table-Mountain Sandstone, but not conformably. The Karoo sandstones and shales occupy the largest portion of South Africa, as they compose the whole of the interior, forming the high elevated plains of the Kalahari, the Free State and the Transvaal, as well as the countries to the north as far up as the Limpopo; they are also to be met with at the Zambezi. As Mr. Tate and Profs. T. R. Jones, Owen, and Huxley have already so ably described this formation with its fossil contents, little remains for me to say. The dark-grey and blue shales of Pietermaritzburg, containing oxide of iron in great quantities, represent the Ecca-beds of the great Karoo. Further up it passes gradually into sandstones of much the same lithological character as the Table-Mountain Sandstone, with intervening layers of shale, which at Dundee, Newcastle, in the Tugela

Valley, &c., contain beds of coal. Numerous remains of reptiles and plants are described, which come from the Natal side of the Drakensberg, and therefore the age of these beds may be determined. Mr. Tate regards them as Triassic, whilst Mr. Wyley thinks that they belong to the Carboniferous period; but as the coal from Tulbagh, in the Cape Colony, is decidedly carboniferous (*Calamites*, *Equisetum*, and *Lepidodendron* in the sandstone), and the succeeding Karoo formation (which is a fresh water deposit) does not lie conformably on the former, Mr. Tate's opinion seems the most acceptable. Also the same formation, with *Dicynodon* and *Glossopteris Browniana* occurring in India at the base of the Cretaceous series, is proved by a careful examination of its flora, to be a Triassic deposit. There can certainly not be the slightest doubt that the Natal coal belongs to a far younger period than the Tulbagh coal, which is an equivalent of the English coal-measures.

The "Karoo formation" also occurs in a small belt on the sea coast of Natal, which belt is never broader than from seven to eight miles, if so much. Beds of the Karoo series are well exposed at the Umgeni mouth and also at the Ifumi River. Any one who has been to Pietermaritzburg must have observed cuttings on the road, about seven or eight miles before he reaches the capital, in a dark shaly rock, with large boulders of older rocks imbedded, of granite, gneiss, slate, and also frequently of greenstone. These boulders are so characteristic of African scenery that they have received general attention. They are often of very large size, and are embedded in a soft grit and shaly clay, containing small particles of mica.

They seem to have been formed on the spot, or at least have not travelled very far, as many of them have retained their angular shape, and they seem to have undergone rather a process of decomposition than of rolling. These beds ("boulder-beds") extend often over a very large area, and pass everywhere beneath the dark shale which represents the base of the Karoo plant-beds. This is proved by a section at Thornville, and also on the sea coast of Natal at several places, amongst them at the Umgeni Valley and the Ifumi River.

Both these sections show that the plant-bearing shales and sandstones rest unconformably on the older Table-Mountain Sandstone, and also that the boulder-bed lies at the base of these plant-beds.

The same is shown at part of the road between Pietermaritzburg and Thornville.

The boulder-bed here, in the same way as in other sections, passes gradually into the shale of Pietermaritzburg, which, it is thought, belongs to the lowest bed of the Karoo series. We learn from the Geological Survey of India that almost the same formation of shales, sandstones and calcareous grit contains the same forms of plants, as well as reptilian remains of *Dicynodon*, and lies conformably on a boulder-bed, which gives the impression that it was formed on the spot, and was not transported by the action of the water. It is also remarkable, and an observed fact, that this boulder-bed of Southern India passes gradually into the succeeding shales and sandstones, which have been termed by the Indian geologists "the Ootatoor plant-beds." A lithologically similar boulder-formation I have also seen at the same horizon in the Cape Colony, passing beneath the blue Karoo shales; and I am pretty certain that Mr. Bain and many African geologists have taken this boulder-bed, at many localities, for an igneous trappean rock. Mr. Bain calls this boulder-bed, which dips under the "Ecca-beds" of the "Pataties Revier," "Claystone Porphyry." There is certainly a basaltic melaphyre, forming beds of considerable extent in this lowest part of the Karoo formation, as can be seen, for instance, near Platte-fontein, in the Karoo; but this trap does not belong to the extensive beds of boulders at the base of the "Pataties Revier" shale. At first sight the trap and the boulder-bed have many similarities, as the material of the boulder is partly derived from igneous rocks. Dr. Sutherland thinks that the boulder-bed was formed by glacial action, and tries to prove it by the observed fact of grooves and furrows on the plateaux of the Table-Mountain Sandstone. These grooves, quite similar to those in the Alps, occur in great abundance on the sandstone of the Ifumi River, about twenty miles south of Durban.

The greenstone (melaphyre?) has found its way through this formation at many places, and forms beds between the strata of it. The greenstone contains a great quantity of pebbles of older rocks imbedded, which give it a speckled appearance. But it seems that the greenstone eruption happened at the earliest period of the forming of the Karoo beds, as the "kopjes" of greenstone are only found in the lowest strata of the "Pietermaritzburg shales," and in the succeeding sandstones. The series of greenstone "kopjes," which runs from the Ingeli Range in Kafirland up through Richmond, York and Greytown to the Tugela River, is of practical importance, as in it, or in the direction of its strike, the occurrence of copper ores can be traced through the whole of South Africa. Besides this Trappean greenstone, a second igneous formation may be found within the Karoo series, the so-called imygdaloid rock, which caps many of the heights of the upper Karoo beds, and often forms extensive beds between them. From it are derived the various kinds of chalcedony, agates, rock-crystals and topazes which are so plentiful in the rivers of the Free State and Natal.

The Cretaceous Rocks of South Africa.—Between the rivers Umtamfuna and Umzambane, about five miles from the southern boundary-line of Natal, some deposits are found which at first sight seem to be of the same material as the underlying stratum. They consist of sandy marls and hard sandstones of a greyish-brown colour, with a few calcareous concretions. These rocks are partly covered at high water by the sea, which has hollowed out small cavities in them. They have probably served at some period as a shelter for white people, as the natives of this district call them "Izinhluzabalungu"—houses of the white men. These rocks only extend for a short distance, and only form isolated cliffs. They are found, too, at the Impengati River, and at some of the more southern rivulets which run into the sea between the boundary of Natal and the St. John's River (Umzimvubu). The same are also recognised in the bed of a small stream running into the St. Lucia Bay, in the Zulu country. The strata forming these deposits are perfectly

Umzimvubu River.

horizontal, and they rest upon a sandstone of much greater age, which belongs to the very interesting series of the Karoo formation. It is remarkable that the Izinhluzabalungu rocks do not rest conformably upon the older formation, the plant-bearing sandstones.

I have been enabled to distinguish no fewer than five distinct faunas. The lowest stratum is a hard calcareous sandstone, very much worn by the sea breaking against it at high water. Large trees and branches are imbedded in it, lying about in all directions. The wood is traversed by large masses of *Teredo*, whose holes are filled with iron pyrites. Resting on this stratum is a bed of softer brown sandstone, with great abundance of *Trigoniæ*. This bed is more exposed near the Umzambane River, and nearly concealed at the northern end of the deposits. It is overlain by sandstones and grits, containing ammonites, resting upon which is a softer sandstone and grit, containing many fossils, mostly bivalves and gasteropods. The roof of the cave is formed by a harder limestone stratum, which has not been so easily worn away by the sea as the underlying sandstone stratum. This limestone contains *Ammonites Gardeni*.

It is quite clear that most of the species obtained from this African locality ("Izinhluzabalungu") resemble in every respect those of the Trichinopoly series of India. The Trigonia bed with *Ammonites Kayei*, *A. Rembda*, &c., show the true character of the Ootatoor beds of the Trichinopoly district, whilst we have the Trichinopoly group represented by eighteen species, which also occur in India. The Arrialoor group is proved only by *Ammonites Gardeni*, which was first described from Africa, but has since been found by Stoliczka in the Indian Cretaceous series.

The plant-beds with *Teredo* find their representative in the lower beds of the Ootatoor group of the Trichinopoly district; and from this, and also the fact that the preceding plant-bearing Karoo formation finds its analogue in the Indian Ootatoor plant-beds (not the Ootatoor group) the conclusion is easy to arrive at, that both Africa and India were, after the development of the Table-Mountain Sandstone, one continuous continent, which afterwards was covered by the Cretaceous sea.

Between the deposition of the Table-Mountain Sandstone and that of the plant-bearing blue shales and of their boulder-bed, from the base of the extensive *Dicynodon* sandstones, a long time must have elapsed.

The large area now covered by the Indian Ocean must have been the basin for an extensive series of lakes, which would explain the occurrence of the same plants and large reptiles which were then living in India and also in South Africa. It must have been a period of long-enduring tranquillity, and no great disturbance whatever seems to have occurred. These periods of repose, which witnessed so very few changes during the deposition of at least 5,000 feet thickness of strata, must have lasted through the Triassic age right up to the Upper Jurassic; as in India the highest of these beds seem to belong to the Jurassic formation. The greater portion of the Indian Ocean must, at this period, have been depressed, together with a large part of India and South Africa, which were covered with the shallow Cretaceous sea, having a peculiar fauna of its own. The Cretaceous deposits of Southern India and Africa were all shallow-water and coast deposits, as is proved by the species of fossils they contain and also by the quantities of wood imbedded in them, which give evidence of a formation on a shallow coast, where the wood was soon covered with sand and mud and in this way preserved. Since that period the coast has been gradually rising, or the sea retiring. The portions of the Cretaceous sea nearest the old coast-line had become dry land; and we see the remains of these deposits in Southern India and South Africa, from the Cape to Durban Bluff, and still further north, even as far as Zanzibar, modern raised beaches, coral-reefs, and oyster-banks may everywhere be seen. At the Izinhluzabalungu Caves there is such a point, where the rising of the coast is plainly visible; recent oyster-banks are now twelve feet and more above high-water mark. The same can be observed on nearly the whole line of the Natal coast. Van der Decken has observed the same thing at Zanzibar, and is of the same opinion as myself, viz., that the eastern coast is rising. Early in 1878 I had the opportunity of observing at the Bazaruto Islands, about 90 miles to the north of Inhambane, on the east coast of Africa, a series of raised coral-reefs round the island of Marsha, containing many living shells and quite recent oyster-banks. In fact, I believe that the Bazaruto Islands only owe their existence to the circumstance that the coral-reefs have been upheaved, and that their surface was naturally covered with loose sea-sand, which is the only soil of the desolate islands. Everywhere, at about 12 to 14 feet depth, water is to be obtained at Marsha; wherever the sand is removed the coral-rock is reached.

If we take a vertical section of the Natal formations, we shall find them as follows :—

- Brown soft sandstones and grit, with great numbers of fossils (Cretaceous series, lower greensand up to white chalk).
- Sandstones and shales, with coalbeds, shales and boulder-bed (greenstone dykes) (Karoo formation, probably Trias, reaching as far as the Jura).
- Quartzose sandstone with shales, containing only traces of fossil remains (Table Mountain sandstone, Coal period).
- Clay and talcose slates, mica-schists, dykes of diorite (Primary slate formation).
- Granite and gneiss, dykes of diorite (Primary rocks).

Within the past two years, gold in payable quantities has been discovered in Natal, both in the northern and southern districts. As yet, of course, no extensive workings have been carried out, but there can be no manner of doubt about the stability and extent of the formations and deposits. Vast beds of coal are also being rapidly developed in several of the up-country districts; while lead, silver, galena, copper and asbestos have been traced in all directions. All that is required is a systematic prospect of the country by men of experience, and the publication of their reports in order to secure the recognition of the country as a mineral one.

CHAPTER VIII.

THE UMZIMKULU RIVER AND PORT SHEPSTONE—SCOTBURG AND UMZINTO.

BOUT sixty miles down the coast, to the southward of Durban, is situated a broad open and navigable river, which, by the enterprise of a small number of Colonists, assisted now and again by a Government vote, has been transformed into a snug little harbour and seaport. It forms an attractive holiday resort, and is of considerable economic importance, both as a port and as an agency for the development of the adjacent inland districts. The distance is traversed by small coasting steamers in eight or ten hours, at a cost to passengers of thirty shillings or thereabouts. On arrival off the Port, one is struck by the tameness and apparent monotony of the coast; but let us not be in haste to condemn, for beyond those low round aloe-studded hills, there lies a rich pastoral and beautiful district. Here and there along the shore, masses of forbidding rock crop up out of the sand; one of these possesses considerable historic interest. It appears that in the olden days of barbaric rule, when the country was full of witchcraft and superstition, the sable potentates who ruled the land were wont to execute their grim justice on evil doers by casting them into a long, narrow and dark fissure in the rocks here. Afterwards, when I looked down into it, and saw the sea foam churned white and fleecy as wool, I could not but conjure up

CROSSING A DRIFT. Road to the Umzinto, Natal.
(From a Photograph by Robert Harris.)

The Union Steam Ship Company, Limited.

the awful spectacle of the frantic and useless struggles of the condemned in their living tomb. The jet-black rocks, the thunder of the sea and the flying spray, were fitting accompaniments to the screams and wails of the luckless criminals.

On the same side of the river, whose mouth is here, is a wooded hill sloping down to a plain, where in days to come, there is no doubt, a city will stand. On the other, or southern side of the river entrance, there is a long, low grassy point, which, as it sweeps inland, rises to an altitude of about three hundred feet. Here are situated the signal station, look-out stand and Port Captain's office. Behind it lies the tiny and scattered village of Umzimkulu.

The river, which at this point forms a broad lagoon, is of an average depth of fifteen feet, and has an open channel leading into the sea—through which small steamers can enter with ease. The view, after entering the lagoon, is very beautiful. Stretching away for miles inland lies the broad still stream, flashing with ripples and flecked with light and shade. On the right-hand side, the mountains come close up to the river edge; while on the left they stand back, leaving a broad strip of rich alluvial plain, which is dotted here and there with the tiny houses of the settlers, of whom there are about 600 in the vicinity.

Taking a boat kindly placed at my disposal by Mr. D. C. Aiken, one of the leading spirits of the locality, I was rowed up stream for seven or eight miles, to the first rapids. This spot, overshadowed as it is on the one hand by dark rich forests, and on the other by St. Helen's Rock, which is a veritable fernery, forms one of the sights of the place. Very little engineering skill will remove the rapids, which are only caused by the sudden narrowing of the river bed by some large boulders. Having surmounted this obstacle, we passed on for another mile or so, obtaining, *en route*, a delightful glimpse of the Umzimkulwana River, which is a tributary of the main stream. Here the forests increase in density, and the hills in height; bright-plumaged birds flitted to and fro, while black-faced monkeys chattered and yelled at us from the security of their native branches. Towards evening we approached the great marble deposits, which were mentioned in the geological report on the Colony. They are located in a grand valley, encompassed by lofty mountains. The outcrop is about one hundred feet above the sea level, and the continuation of the strata can be traced on the opposite side of the river. After spending the night in the forest, where we rested on a snow-white marble floor, under a canopy of drooping branches, through which the myriad stars peeped like jewels, the return journey was undertaken. At every turn of the river fresh beauties greeted us ; and as the boat sped on, borne by the force of the river, we saw the dizzy height where a bee-hunter, but a short time before, had met with his death while taking a hive. It appears that he got wedged amongst the rocks, and while in that position was stung to death by the insects.

In the very near future, Umzinkulu is certain to become a place of considerable commercial importance, for it is the natural outlet for the trade of all the southern districts of Natal.

Of the other ports along the Natal coast, Umkomanzi, Scotburg and Umzinto are the only ones which can be reasonably expected to advance much. They tap the country at rich and well-populated points; sugar, rum, hides, waggon wood, and maize are the principal exports to be expected from them, though, when matters are further advanced, a host of others may be added.

CHAPTER IX.

The Orange River Free State and Basutoland.

WHEN dealing with Kimberley and Griqualand West, mention was made of the British Orange River Sovereignty, which has since become the Orange Free State. Its area, as accurately as can be ascertained, is fifty thousand square miles. It is bounded on the north-west and north by the Vaal River, which separates it from the Transvaal or South African Republic; on the east by the Drakensberg Mountains, which separate it from Natal; on the south-east by the Caledon River and an irregular line which separates it from Basutoland; on the south by the Orange River, which separates it from the Cape Colony. Its population at present (1889) may be about 90,000, more than half of whom are coloured.

The history of the country is in a sense the history of Natal and the Cape Colony. According to the most ancient records, it was originally peopled by a race called Bushmen (Bosjesmen), which were—and such as remain are—a detestable and repulsive nation of dwarfs, whose habits are as filthy as their traditions. Armed with bows and arrows, they dwelt in caves and holes, caring neither to clothe themselves nor build dwellings. Their chief occupation in life was to rob their neighbours and maltreat all who, by an evil chance, fell into their power. These were displaced by a cross-bred race, called Griquas, who being better armed, drove them into the fastness of the mountains, whence they swooped down on any stray herds that came within reach. Following the original Griquas came the Basutos, under their veteran chief Moshesh, whose head-quarters were in the mountain ranges between the Orange and the Caledon Rivers. While these worthies were wrangling over the land, the overflowing and restless population of the Cape Colony began to creep out over the great plains and establish themselves here and there.

Then came the exodus of Boers of 1835-6-7, from the Cape Colony on their way to colonise Natal; some of these dropped out doubtless, for after their passage some new names crop up in the early history of the place. It is extremely difficult at this stage to avoid confusion, for we have four rival races struggling for territory, *i.e.*, the English at the Cape and Natal, the Dutch, the Basutos, and the Griquas. The Basutos very soon returned to their much-loved mountains and left the Dutch and Griquas to squabble to their heart's content.

It was at this period (1845) that the English first took a hand in the game, by appointing an officer to keep order. Sir Peregrine Maitland's idea was to assume authority and control the land and yet allow it to remain as it was, a sort of Tom Tiddler's ground for all sorts of malcontents. Peace was an unknown blessing, and war was every man's business. At this stage, Sir Harry Smith arrived in South Africa. Very shortly afterwards (February 3rd, 1848) he issued a proclamation extending British Sovereignty over the region lying between the Orange and Vaal Rivers. By this course he hoped to end the strife that had for some years reigned throughout the land; at the same time he had no intention of disturbing the native chiefs or wresting their land from them.

At this period a Boer leader, named Pretorius, rallied the emigrant Dutchmen round him, and the result was open revolt, which led to several battles, after which the English established themselves as masters. Peace now promised to reign instead of disorder, when some ill-advised persons in England succeeded in persuading the Government to abandon the territory to the emigrants. This was done on the 23rd of February, 1854.

For a number of years wars and rumours of wars disturbed the new State. The Basutos proved formidable foemen to it. On the 12th of March, 1868, the English interfered by declaring the Basutos to be under the protection of the British Empire; and in 1869 a definite boundary was fixed. The present prosperity and stability of the Free State is to be mainly attributed to the wise and statesmanlike policy pursued by the late Sir John Brand, who, until 1888, filled the position of President of the Republic with credit to himself and his country, and with advantage to the rest of South Africa.

The principal towns in the State are, Bloemfontein (River of Flowers), Smithfield, Bethulie, Fauresmith, Harrismith, Winburg, and Kronstad. Besides these there are several hamlets. The official language of the country is Dutch, though English (owing to the number of British colonists) is generally understood and used. But little land remains in the hands of the Government, it being nearly all parcelled out in farms.

Geographically, the country consists of an immense plain, sloping slightly and continuously towards the west. The Caledon, which runs into the Orange, and the Reit and Modder, which unite near the western boundary line, are the main streams of the country. The country is well governed, and English settlers, tourists and travellers are as much at home in it as though under their own flag.

There are thirteen divisions in the State, as follows :— Boshof, Winburg, Kronstad, Harrismith, Jacobsdal, Fauresmith, Bloemfontein, Smithfield, Phillipolis, Bethulie, Rouxville, Bethlehem and Ladybrand. Most praiseworthy and successful progress has been made in the Educational Department of the State. Owing to the scattered population, large and important schools are almost an impossibility. At Bloemfontein, the capital, and in the other centres, good plain schools are established. The Government contributes largely to their maintenance, and encourages educational advances of every kind. Most of the wealthier Boers employ private tutors

G

or governesses. The Dutch "Reformed" is the State Church, and the majority of the population attend it. Missionary enterprise is well represented by several denominations. The revenues of the State are chiefly derived from quit-rents, land transfer dues, licenses, and hut taxes levied on the natives.

British Basutoland was, as we have just seen, brought under British rule in 1868. It is bounded by the Cape Colony, the Orange River Free State, Griqualand East and Natal, and is composed of the watersheds of the Caledon and Orange Rivers. Here it was that the grand old mountain chief, Moshesh, held his own, and no more, against all comers, and here it is that the missionary enterprise amongst native Africans has met with most success. The country, since its annexation to the British Empire, has been divided into magistracies, as follows: Leribe, Thaba-Bosigo, Berea and Cornet-Spruit. The population has been put down at 127,700 souls, but my impression is that there are considerably more than that number now. In each of the magistracies there is a European administrator, and over them is an officer with the title of Commissioner. The hereditary chiefs have considerable power, but are not allowed to inflict death or other severe sentences. The clans of Basutoland are members of the Bechuana tribes, speak a kindred language, and have similar customs. They at present are the best advanced, and, in my opinion, the most intelligent tribe in South Africa. As a proof of this, we may point to the fact that each year a larger quantity of grain is raised than they can consume; with this surplus they purchase European luxuries and manufactures. I have been told that, in 1880, seven hundred thousand bushels of wheat, maize and millet, together with two thousand, or over, bales of wool, were traded for blankets, cottons, &c. There are about fifty trading stations established in this country, and property is respected by them. Considering the number of the tribe, there is but little crime. Stock comprises their chief wealth, and in 1875 the census returns showed them to be possessed of 35,357 horses, 217,732 head of horned cattle,

The Union Steam Ship Company, Limited.

303,080 sheep, 215,485 goats, 299 waggons, and 2,749 ploughs. Physically, they are a tall, robust set of men, with bluff, boldly-cut faces, very dark, and possessed of bright, intelligent eyes. The present native rulers of this sturdy nation are Letsie, and Jonathan and Joel Malapo.

It would be an aimless task to reproduce the story of the petty wars which have from time to time rent the country; the fact that at present it is in a peaceable and prosperous condition, and that year by year the natives are winning their way to civilisation and its attendant blessings, is sufficient. From a picturesque point of view, Basutoland is unique; steppe piled on steppe, and mountain on mountain, meet the eye in all directions. When, in the course of time, our great artists have wearied of their everlasting journeys to the Rhinelands, Italy, and other continental beauty spots, we may hope to hear a joyful shout of delight at the grand and noble scenes which, touched by their magic brushes, will yet adorn the walls of our Academies of Arts.

CHAPTER X.

BRITISH BECHUANALAND.

EFORE proceeding to the Transvaal, and the native states adjoining it, we will take a passing peep into the vast new region which has so recently been added to British South Africa. Bechuanaland lies to the west and north of the Transvaal Republic, and between it and the so-called Kalahari Desert. It was formerly under the government of a number of chiefs, of whom Mankoroane was the principal amongst the Batlapins, and Montsida amongst the Baralongs. The former chief, on the 3rd of May, 1884, surrendered his territories into the hands of the British Government. A few days later, Montsida did likewise. The boundaries of the region are described as west of the South African Republic, north of the Colony of the Cape of Good Hope, east of the 20th meridian of east longitude, and south of the 22nd parallel of south latitude.

On the 23rd of March, 1885, a formal proclamation was issued announcing it as a British protectorate. On the 30th of September in the same year, it was announced that that portion of the Protectorate which is bounded on the east by the Transvaal, on the south by the Cape Colony, on the west by the Molopo River, and on the north by the same river to its junction with the Ramathlabana Spruit, and thence by the said Spruit to the frontier of the Republic, should be thenceforward called British Bechuanaland. The area of the country is about 180,000 square miles, with a population of 1,000 whites and 200,000 natives.

These latter are of kindred race with the Kafirs further to the north and east, and like them, form distinct clans or tribes which are governed by hereditary chiefs. Their language is similarly formed, but without the clicks of the Zulu and Amaponda tongues.

At one time they occupied the region now known as the Transvaal; but when the chief Moselekatsie revolted from the army of Chaka, and burst into the country, carrying slaughter and death with him, they fell back to their present country and settled there, flanked by the desert on one hand, and by blood-thirsty foemen on the other.

Although the Bechuanas are not so robust and warlike as the Zulus, they are much more ingenious and skilful in the manufacture of domestic utensils, clothing, implements, and weapons. Their huts are more commodious than those of the coast tribes, the roofs being lofty and very thick. Their religion is similar to that of the Zulus, and will be dealt with in due course. Missionaries (chief amongst whom may be mentioned the well-known names of Moffat, Livingstone, and John McKenzie) have for many years toiled among them, and in the writings of the two latter, much valuable information is to be gleaned.

The climate of Bechuanaland is remarkably salubrious, being, as Dr. Livingstone puts it, "the complete antipodes of cold damp England." The winters are perfectly dry and bracing.

In the opinion of those who know the country best, Bechuanaland has a grand future before it, as a field for European emigration. I have the kind permission of the Rev. Mr. McKenzie, one of the veteran missionaries whom I have cited as an acknowledged and undisputed authority on the land, to quote the following passage from his recent work entitled *Austral Africa*—

" I come now to give my own thoughts as to the capabilities of Bechuanaland as a field for colonisation. My mind reverts to thrifty and laborious people who are battling for dear life on some small holding in England or Scotland, and who can barely make ends meet. I do not think that any class of men, or men of any colour, endure such hardship in South Africa. There are portions of Bechuanaland where, in my opinion, a body of some hundreds of agricultural emigrants would take root from the first, and make for themselves homes. If they came in considerable numbers, and accompanied by a minister of religion and possibly a schoolmaster, the children would not be losers by the change, while the church and the school-house would form that centre in South Africa, with which all are familiar in Scotland. I would not suggest that such men should be merely agriculturists, but that like most farmers in South Africa they should follow both branches of farming. They would begin with some sheep, or a few goats and a few cows. In the first instance they would have a freehold in the village and a right to pasturage, and they would also have the farm itself in the neighbourhood, the size of which would depend on its locality and capabilities. But with the milk of the stock and the produce of the land in maize, millet and pumpkins, he and his family would be, from the first, beyond the reach of want."—*Austral Africa*, Vol. ii, p. 356.

CHAPTER XI.

THE TRANSVAAL REPUBLIC.

IN the last section mention was made of the invasion, by Moselekatse, of the vast region that lies between the Limpopo in the north, the Vaal River in the south, the Drakensberg Mountains in the east and the Kalahari in the west. The old Lion of the North, as Moselekatse was commonly called, built up a powerful state here, partly by the splendid organisation of his own warriors and partly by a wise mingling of them with the defeated races. Parties of Griquas, trusting to their guns, attacked him at the time of the Orange River emigration, but he beat them off; then, gaining courage by success, he sent out marauding parties to scour the country and make what they could. In one of these excursions, it will be remembered, they met the emigrant Boers and inflicted heavy losses on them. These sturdy pioneers made haste to carry war into his country, and in revenge for the death of their brethren succeeded in shattering his power, capturing 7,000, or more, head of cattle and driving him back to the region now called Matabeleland, where the tribe under King Lo Bengula are at present located. The Lion of the North ceased to roar in the region beyond the Vaal; the white settlers flocked in and spread themselves over the whole land, some going even as far north as the Limpopo.

Although these settlers were ready enough to help each other and unite against a common foe, there was unhappily no organisation amongst them, and at first no attempt was made to set up an independent government. Matters remained in this unsettled condition until 1848, when Andries Pretorious put in an appearance. Immediately he was invested with supreme military command over all the emigrants in the region. A government was established similar to that which had just fallen at Natal. During the years 1849-50-51, constant streams of English-hating emigrant Boers kept drifting in, so that the central and southern parts of the district began to be fairly well populated; though, as each farmer owned about 10,000 acres, we cannot regard them as in any way crowded. It appeared at last that they had attained the goal of their happiness, *i.e.*, freedom from English control, for by this time the British authorities had begun to realise that it was of little use to attempt ruling so turbulent and rugged a community. They had all Africa at their backs, and openly boasted that if interfered with again, they would not hesitate to plunge still deeper into the heart of the continent. Accordingly, on the 17th January, 1852, they were formally recognised by the established Governments on the coast.

Shortly after this, Pretorious, worn out with cares of state, died, and in him they lost their grandest champion and leader. For about fifteen years after this event, matters drifted on slowly and quietly in the Transvaal, as the region was now called. The discovery of diamonds to the south, and the almost equally important Lydenburg Gold Fields to the north of the Republic, caused a regular but small stream of traffic to spring up in the land, for the connecting roads crossed the very heart of the country. Settlers from Europe and from the adjacent colonies came slowly in; newspapers in English were established and published at both Pretoria and Potchefstroom. These advances caused, in a short time, a change of policy, and old obstructional ideas gave place to progressive ones. The President, Mr. Burgers, was despatched to Europe for the purpose of raising £300,000, on the security of five hundred farms, of six thousand acres each, the intention being to lay down a railway to Delagoa Bay, on the east coast.

The negotiations, though promising fairly at first, ultimately failed, but not before a loss of something like £90,000 was inflicted on the struggling Government. Some few years after this, owing to the deplorably bankrupt condition of the country, England, on the request of a section of the community, formally annexed the country and appointed a Government; but this did not meet the views of the majority, who, in 1881, broke into open revolt, and succeeded in regaining their national independence. Since then marvellous deposits of gold have been discovered in the land, and the revenues accruing to the State from licences, &c., have set it on a permanent and secure footing.

Geographically, the Transvaal is closely akin to the Orange Free State and Bechuanaland, it being composed, for the most part, of vast open and almost treeless plains. One of its principal rivers is the Oliphant, which takes its rise in the Magaliesbergen, and flows in a northerly direction at first, then sweeping round to the east, finds a passage through the Drakensberg to the sea. Along its course, it is joined by a countless number of smaller streams.

The scenery of the Transvaal is grand and inspiring in certain parts, particularly in the east, where the country is torn into jagged mountain ranges. The area of the Transvaal has been set down at 114,000 square miles, and the population as follows :—whites, 65,000, natives at 700,000.

CHAPTER XII.

EARLY ACCOUNTS OF GOLD IN AFRICA.—MONOMOTAPA.

HERE cannot be a shadow of doubt that Africa, from the most remote periods, has been a gold-producing country. While travelling on the east coast, in the vicinity of Sofala, in 1883-4-5, I found numerous traces of long-abandoned workings, while the fact that many Hebrew customs, and even manners, are extant to this day in the land, taken in conjunction with the statements made by Josephus in his *Antiquities of the Jews*, all point to the identity of South-East Africa with the Ophir of the Scriptures. Traditions are also to be heard amongst the natives, to the effect that many thousand years ago, ships from a far-off land came regularly in quest of the "yellow metal" and the hard woods indigenous to the country.

The following are a few of the reasons for supposing South-East Africa to be, in very truth, "King Solomon's Mines":—

Ophir is translated in the earliest Greek versions of the Old Testament as Sophira or Sophara. This bears a striking analogy to the modern Sofala.

The articles Solomon got from Ophir were gold, ivory, apes, and algumim wood—according to Josephus, a white shining wood.

Gold and ivory, we know, have been procured in great quantities in Sofala, as well as apes; and it is remarkable that the Hebrew name of the apes mentioned, namely, "koph," seems to bear some analogy to the name of "kabo," at present used to designate an ape by the tribes to the north.

As regards the algumim wood, it is uncertain what variety is meant. It is generally supposed to be the red sandal-wood of India, of which specimens are also to be found in Africa.

But what Josephus says with regard to this wood is very interesting. In his *Antiquities of the Jews*, book viii, chap. vii, he remarks:—" The wood brought to Solomon (from Ophir) was larger and finer than any that has ever been brought before; but let no one imagine that these pine trees were like those which are now so named, for those we speak of were to the sight like the wood of the fig tree, but whiter and shiny."

According to this statement of Josephus, it is very likely that the algumim wood is the yellow wood, now so familiar to the colonists of South Africa.

He also mentions precious stones brought from Ophir to Solomon, and it is well known that in the vicinity of Sofala rubies and topazes are to be found.

There was a scruple against the belief that Ophir was in Africa, on account of the peacocks which the Ophir ships carried home with them, because there are none of these birds in Africa, but the Ophir traders may have procured them during the voyage, perhaps from some town of Indian trade on the shores of the Red Sea, as it is known that in those times a large trade was carried on between Egypt and India.

The Dominican monk Joao Dos Santos set out in the year 1587 for Mozambique and Sofala, and spent eleven years amongst the different Portuguese settlements in that region. In his *Eastern Ethiopia* (Evora, 1609), among other things he relates the following:—" The merchandise from Tete goes down to Sene with the gold which is brought from the market of Massapa, in the kingdom of Monomotapa, where a large quantity is always to be met with, as the great and lofty mountain Fura (or Afura) is close by. Upon this mountain are to be seen the ruins of buildings constructed of stone and lime—a thing which is not to be found in the whole of the Kafir country, where even the houses of the king are only built of wood and earth, and thatched with straw. An old tradition current in this country affirms that these ruins are the remains of the storehouses of the Queen of Sheba; further, that this princess got all her gold from these mountains, and that this gold was carried down the River Cuama (Zambezi) to the Ethiopian Ocean, and taken thence through the Red Sea to the coasts of Ethiopia above Egypt, where this Queen dwelt. Others believe that Solomon had these magazines built, and that here was obtained that gold of Ophir with which his navies were laden; that between Afura and Ophir there is no great difference. It is quite certain that around this mountain range much and very fine gold is found, easily conveyed by means of this river, as is still done by the Portuguese, and was done before them by the Moors of Mozambique and Kilwa; and further, that as in these days gold is carried to India, so in former days it might easily have been taken through the Red Sea to Ezion-Geber, and thence to Jerusalem."

Carl Ritter, in the first part of his *Erdkunde* (Berlin, 1817), thus sums up the more ancient reports, especially those of the Portuguese :—

"The most remarkable thing told of this district relates to the ancient buildings in the kingdom of Butua, in the country of Toróa, of which De Barros (Dec. I. l. X., c. 1, fol. 118 b.) gives a very minute description. As they will yet serve as a point of comparison between ancient and modern geography, we must by no means pass them over.

"'In the midst of the plain in the kingdom of Butua, near the oldest gold mines, stands a fortress (*fortaleza*), square, admirably built, inside and out, of hard freestone. The blocks of which the walls consist are put together without mortar, and are of extraordinary size (*marauilhose grandeza*). The walls are twenty-five spans in thickness; their height is not so considerable compared with their breadth. Over the gate of the building is an inscription which neither the Moorish traders (that is, the Arab inhabitants of the coast) who were there, nor others learned in inscriptions, could read; nor does any one know in what character it is written. On the heights around this edifice stand others, in like manner built of masonry without mortar; among them a tower of more than twelve *bracas* in height.

"'All these buildings are called by the natives Symbáoe—that is, the royal residence (*Corte*), as are all royal dwellings in Monomotapa. Their guardian, a man of noble birth, has here the chief command, and is called Symbacayo; under his care are some of the wives of the Benomotapa, who constantly reside here. When and by whom these buildings were erected is unknown to the natives, who have no written characters. They say merely that they are the work of the devil, because they are beyond the power of man to execute. When Captain Vic Pegado, with a view to comparison, pointed out the Portuguese masonry of the fort at Sofala, with its windows, vaults, &c., to some Moors who had been at the Ruins, they observed that the latter structure was of such absolute perfection (*limpa y perfecta*) that nothing could be compared with it. These buildings stand in 20 and 21 degrees S. lat., about 170 leagues due west of Sofala. Besides them is to be found no other mason-work, ancient or modern, in that region, seeing that all the dwellings of the barbarian nation there are of wood (*madeira*). In the opinion of the Moors, these buildings are very ancient and erected for the protection of the neighbouring gold mines, which are believed to be the most ancient in the country.'

"From all this De Barros infers that this must be the Agysymba of Ptolemy, founded by an ancient ruler of this gold country who was unable to hold his ground, as in the case of the ruins of Caxum (Axum) in the land of Prester John.

"Dos Santos also says that these are the only massive buildings in Kaffraria; that the Portuguese, however, were not allowed to ascend to Butua, on the heights of Fura, because the whole of Monomotapa was visible thence, lying eastward along the rivers, and therefore on a lower level; and that the districts whence they drew their gold could also be descried thence.

"Battel (in *Purchas's Pilgrimage*) says that the country of the Abutua lies north-west of Monomotapa, stretching out in great plains towards the interior, westward, from the frontier mountain chain, whence the Zambezi and Manica flow eastward. The country falls eastward towards Monomotapa, and westward towards Massapa.

"As on the eastern coasts of Africa among the Arabs and Moors, wherever gold is to be found the Queen of Sheba is met with in the legends of the past as a mighty princess, and as the country of Fura is also called Afura, all this reminds one of Ofir or Ophir, and these (the same tale meeting us again at Axum), remind us of a castle of the Queen of Sheba, whose fleets are said to have conveyed her treasures of gold down the Zambezi to Arabia."

A German explorer, named Mauch, devoted himself to the task of unravelling the mystery; with the result of discovering, in the year 1868, the ruins of the ancient cities or fortresses just described. His reports were forwarded to Dr. Petermann, of Gotha, who summed them up as follows:—

"The Ophir of the Bible from whence King Solomon, nearly 3,000 years ago, imported immense quantities of gold, ivory and precious stones, in Phœnician ships to complete the beautiful buildings in Jerusalem, has eluded search and baffled investigation for many hundred years. Some have sought it in East Africa and South Arabia, others in India or Sumatra, and others in the West Indies and even Peru; but all have come to the like conclusion that rich mines existed somewhere in Africa, from whence gold was obtained. When the Portuguese reached Sofala in the 16th century they found very rich gold mines, which had evidently been worked for uncounted ages, and by the side of these gold excavations they found buildings and ruins which, according to the traditions of the natives, owed their origin to the Queen of Saba (Sheba).

The inhabitants of Sofala, according to Lopez, boasted that they possessed old books which confirmed the expeditions of Solomon to Ophir. The whole of the literature of the Greeks and Romans leaves us in ignorance as to their earlier intercourse of nations, and only so much is certain from the ancient Arabian writers that, after the fall of the Phœnicians, the gold-seeking Arabians carried on the digging in the middle ages; and in their expeditions from the Persian Gulf they went south, frequently visiting the coast of Sofala. The Portuguese rule in Sofala, at present, is but a shadow of what existed in ancient times, and their attempts made in our time to add to their possessions in the interior of Africa by force of arms have only ended in defeat. Rumours had, for a long series of years, reached from time to time the furthest advanced European settlements of the Cape Colony and the Transvaal, of the existence of extensive ruins of temples, obelisks, and pyramids in the far interior of South Africa, and the missionaries of the Berlin society had resolved to clear up the misty legends respecting these things, and to go to investigate, if possible, for themselves. Up to this time they have found this impracticable; but have, nevertheless, materially assisted the German traveller, Carl Mauch, who had already deserved so well, by his former explorations and labours, to carry into effect his long-formed determination to visit these primeval structures. Letters and charts from this indefatigable and distinguished traveller from the Zimbabye, dated 13th September, 1871, have been forwarded to me by the Rev. Messrs. Grützner and Merensky, stating that he had positively found very extensive buildings and ruins of high antiquity. Zimbabye is one of these old ruined cities, and, according to Mauch's astronomical observations, is situated in lat. 20 deg. 14 min. south and long. 31 deg. 48 min. east from Greenwich. It is exactly west from the port of Sofala and only about 41 German miles in a direct line from that place. This coincides with the statement of the writer, Dos Santos, to the effect that the Portuguese had found extensive walls of masonry

200 nautical miles west from Sofala in the gold country (*tracto do ouro*). In the neighbourhood of Zimbabye, Mauch also found alluvial gold. The ruins consist of a tower and walls of heights up to 30 feet, 15 feet thick, and 450 in diameter; they are all, without exception, built of hewn granite, put together without mortar, which, in itself, is a proof that they must be very ancient. Drawings and specimens of ornamentation, &c., sent by Herr Mauch, leave little doubt that they are neither of Arabian nor Portuguese origin, but in all probability wrought by the Phœnicians, to which people the expeditions sent out by Solomon belonged. At all events, the ornamentation has nothing of a Portuguese or Arabic character, but indicates a much earlier time. The people inhabiting this district have only occupied it about forty years, and they consider these ruins sacred. Their belief is that white people have formerly inhabited the country, which appears to be the fact from the remains of dwellings and iron tools, which could not have been the work of the blacks. Mauch had at first been able to visit only one of the ruined cities, and examine it very cursorily. Three days' journey west of Zambabye lie other ruins, which, according to the statement of the natives, among other things, contain an obelisk. Mauch was in hopes thoroughly to explore the whole district, which is very beautiful, with an altitude of 4,000 feet above the sea level, well watered, fruitful, and thickly peopled by an industrious and peaceful race, the Makalaka, who engage in agriculture and cattle breeding, and possess rice and cornfields, cattle, sheep and goats. An expedition, which, from Solomon's ports in the Red Sea, occupied out and home three years, would agree tolerably well, considering the then state of navigation, with a voyage along the eastern coasts of Africa."

The following letters, from the pen of the dauntless and scientific explorer, will, in the light of recent advances, be read with interest, both in England, where the subject is now attracting attention, and in Africa, where it is the absorbing question of the day:—

The Union Steam Ship Company, Limited.

Letter from the Missionary, the Rev. A. Merensky, to A. Petermann.

Botschabelo, 14th November, 1871.

Herewith I send you some slight notes which Mauch has forwarded to me out of the Banyai country. He has found the Ruins upon the Upper Tokwe. For many years past I had made enquiries among the natives regarding these primeval structures. In 1862 I was compelled by various circumstances to abandon the attempt to reach them.* This year I had

---

* In the *Transvaal Argus* of 20th October, 1868, Mr. Merensky relates this attempt as follows:—"In the year 1861 the Missionary Nachtigal and I were instructed by the Missionary Society to proceed on an exploratory journey northward from Sekwati's country, where I then lived. Our first care was to engage guides who knew the country. Having already heard in Germany that great and ancient ruins were to be found in the regions between the Limpopo and the Zambesi, we enquired about them. It surprised us to find that the existence of these Ruins was well-known to the Makwapa (Knopneusen or Knobnoses). Sekukuni, our chief and son of Sekwati, told us that he had himself, when a boy, seen the Ruins. According to his account there was an immense plain, many hours in extent, covered with the remains of gigantic antique structures. In consequence of this information we set out upon our journey. On reaching the country of the Baroka, beyond the Elephant River, we met with a chief of the Makwapa tribe (Knobnoses), who appeared greatly astonished at our knowledge of the Ruins, but at last gave us permission to proceed thither. We had about a dozen people of Sekwati's tribe with us, but engaged in addition some ten Makwapa as carriers and guides. Other natives warned our people that in the attempt to push on to the Ruins we should all be murdered, because the Makwapa were in the habit of procuring different articles thence, and therefore kept them concealed from other tribes. We could not, however, ascertain what these articles were, and continued our journey. A guide of the Banyai tribe, close to whose territory the Ruins are said to be situated, told us much about this mysterious spot, and thus we gathered that the Banyai revere these ancient buildings: that no living creature may there be put to death, no tree destroyed, since everything is considered sacred. He also informed us that a populous black tribe, who were acquainted with the use of firearms, had formerly dwelt there, but on account of the increasing draught had, about fifty years before, gone northwards. We heard many

planned setting out with Mauch for the mysterious North, when I was prevented by a hostile inroad upon my Station. I rejoice that Mauch has found the spot: rejoice too that he was spurred on by the intelligence I had collected to make one more attempt in that direction. There must be other spots in the Banyai where ruins are to be found, and it is to be hoped that he will be enabled to visit them.

I had at an earlier period heard that Makwapa and Moselikatse's people were in the habit of seeking and finding *tsepe*—that is *metal*—near the Ruins. Mauch's statement confirms this. I imagine iron implements to be meant, such as were used in ancient times in the gold mines and there lost. Gold has never been sought for by Moselikatse's people. I much fear it will be a difficult matter to dig inscriptions or the like out of the rubbish.

How often may these ruins have served for a temporary refuge amid the endless feuds of the native races! May not even the Portuguese have somehow made use of them? In any case the ancient Monomotapa will now for many years furnish material for research to travellers and to the learned.

1.—*Letter from C. Mauch to A. Petermann.*

Santsha, Lat. 20° 15′ S., Long. 31° 37¼′ E., 4,200 feet absolute height above the Sea.

13th September, 1871.

From Zoutpansberg I sent you through the Rev. Messrs. Grützner and Merensky my last maps and reports, and by a favourable opportunity have now the pleasure of forwarding you later intelligence. I can, however, only give you very briefly the results of my journey thus far, the relation of which

---

details regarding the form and construction of these ancient piles and the inscriptions they bore, but I cannot answer for their truth. We were at length compelled to return without having seen the spot, for the tribes we met with were suffering from a virulent epidemic of smallpox, and our people fearing contagion refused to proceed further."

will however convince you how fruitful beyond expectation the journey will prove.

Having on the 30th July taken my departure from Albasini's, with fewer bearers however than I required, I met with an involuntary detention of several days from rain at Sewaas's (Umswazi's) where my goods got considerably reduced in apparently the most amiable manner possible. Through the same friendliness on the part of Umswazi, my companions on the Bembe were not fewer than forty in number, all of whom on account of the prevalent scarcity of game looked to me for food. On the 12th August we passed the Bubye, on the 16th the Nuanetsi, and on the 18th August arrived at Dumbo's Kraal.

I now hired some of Dumbo's people, who subsequently stole from me three bales of calico and a variety of other articles, and then left me quite alone. The people of the kraal being Makalaka, I could not come to an understanding with them. I was again plundered to a considerable extent, but the booty was brought back the same day. At the kraal of Mapansule I encountered a band of Amaswazi warriors who would fain have detained me.

On the 3rd September discovered the first gold field, and on the 5th September discovered the ruins of Zimbabye, probably the Zimbaoe of the Portuguese. Several other points of importance, historical and economic, present themselves in immediate prospect.

After so many depredations my goods were now reduced to a few beads and copper rings. Owing to the extremely populous character of the country, with kraal set against kraal, my expenses are necessarily great in order to make friends with all. The advanced season of the year will not allow of my making more extensive excursions, and I must be content to take up my abode here during the summer months, if for no other reason than this, that I can on no account venture to proceed further until I am able to speak the native language. I am forced in the greatest possible haste to send people to

Zoutpansberg to bring back more goods; and they will have to make stiff marches daily to return within a month. But this costs money, and unfortunately not a little; and I shall be hard put to it to raise the amount required. I see no other means but that of drawing upon you and asking you to have the goodness to honour my draft. I confidently rely on being able during the summer months to wash gold enough to ward off want.

A traveller, named Adam Render, who represents me as being a distinguished chief and has warmly taken up my cause, will be my companion on my further journey.

Zimbaoe, known through Portuguese works, lies 11 English miles east from here and presents an immense fortress, consisting of two portions, of which the one, situated upon a hill some 400 feet in height with huge fragments of rock, is separated by a narrow valley from the second which stands upon a gentle rise. It has hitherto been impossible for me to make a plan of these two Ruins as the walls, in many places still 30 feet in height, are covered up, and formidable plants of the nettle kind would sharply repay any rash attempt to effect a passage. The walls are built without mortar, of hewn granite blocks, about the size of our bricks, enclosing an area of about 150 yards in diameter, and in excellent preservation except at three points.

In the southerly portion is a tower about thirty feet in height, cylindrical in form below and conical higher up. In the advanced wall are several black stones inserted, which I conjecture to indicate a burial-place. As already stated, the vegetation is so rank that but little can be observed on a hasty visit. Not until some future time shall I be in a position to give more detailed information.

Gold Field No. 1, of 1871, is only half-an-hour northward from here, and the people of the kraal are quite willing to engage in gold-washing at a fitting time.

I would fain write more to-day, but a stiff march from Zimbaoe hither in a furious south-east wind has caused me violent headache, and my messengers are anxious to start at the earliest hour to-morrow morning. You must for this time, therefore, please to take the will for the deed—my diary will prove all the richer for it. With the exception of the Bubye, I have taken the width of every stream I have crossed.

Bembe (Limpopo) 22° 18′ 49″ S. lat.—250 yds. wide, 3 ft. deep, 1,780 feet above the sea.
Nuanetsi............ 21 29 47   ,,   —150 yds. wide, but little water.
Dumbo's Kraal ... 21   4 19   ,,
Tokwe River ...... 20 39 58   ,,
Pike's Kraal ...... 20 15 34   ,,   —31° 37′ 45″ E. long.; 4,200 ft. above the sea.

11.—*Letter from G. Mauch to Rev. Mr. Gruetzner.*

Pike's Kraal, 13th September, 1871.

A good God has guided me wonderfully during the month of August and the early part of September. Zimbaoe, or Zimbabye, lies 3½ miles to the south from the above point, my present abode, and consequently in long. 31° 48′ E., and lat. 20° 14′ S. From the inhabitants settled here I learnt that they have only lived here for about forty years: that previously the district had been left quite uninhabited, and that still earlier the Malotse or Barotse lived in the country and near the Ruins, but were compelled to flee northward. These last had regarded the Ruins as sacred, and even now people are said to come in order to worship there. To ascertain the object of this reverence was, however, on account of the superstitions fears of the inhabitants, impossible. On all hands it is accepted as certain that white men have formerly peopled this country, for there are constantly traces met with of dwellings and of iron implements which could not have been the handiwork of blacks. What has become of this white population—whether driven out, killed, or dead of pestilence—no man can tell. On a hasty visit to the very widely-spread parts of these Ruins, I was not able (by the removal of rubbish and frag-

ments of stone) to light upon any inscriptions. I picked up
no implements which would enable one to determine the age
of the Ruins; many, indeed all that could be laid hands upon,
had been consumed by the present occupants of the country;
the Barotse are said to have touched nothing. Had these
Ruins been founded by the Portuguese, they would certainly
have given the place a Portuguese name, as was their custom
everywhere; they must, then, have found these buildings
already erected, and possibly have somewhat altered them.

The Ruins may be divided into two parts: the one upon a
granite rocky eminence of 400 feet in height, the other upon a
somewhat elevated terrace. The two are separated by a
gentle valley, their distance apart being about 300 yards. The
rocky bluff consists of an elongated mass of granite rounded in
form, upon which stands a second block, and upon this again
fragments, smaller, but still many tons in weight, with fissures,
chasms and cavities. The western side of this mountain is
covered from top to bottom by the Ruins. As they are for the
most part fallen in and covered with rubbish, it is at present
impossible to determine the purpose the buildings were in-
tended to serve: the most probable supposition is that it was
a fortress impregnable in those times, and this the many
passages—now, however, walled up—and the circular or zigzag
plan of the walls would also indicate. All the walls, without
exception, are built without mortar, of hewn granite, more or
less about the size of our bricks; the walls, too, are of varying
thickness—at the apparent foot about ten feet thick, at the
ruined top from seven to eight feet. The most remarkable of
the walls is one situated on the edge of a precipitous cliff, and
which, strange to say, is in perfect preservation to a height of
about thirty feet.

In many places there remain beams of stone eight or ten
feet in length, projecting from the walls, in which they must
be inserted to a depth of several feet, for they can scarcely be
stirred. At the most they are eight inches broad by three
inches in thickness, and consist of a very compact stone with

a metallic ring and of greenish-black colour. I found one stone beam, ellipsoid in section and eight feet in length, upon which ornaments are engraved. The ornaments consist chiefly of lozenge-shaped figures one within another, separated by horizontal bands of diagonal lines. Under a great mass of rock I found a broken vessel, shaped like a wooden Kafir-basin, of talcose gneiss, extremely soft, eighteen inches in diameter and three inches deep; one and a-half inch in thickness at the edge and half an inch thick in the bottom. Nothing else could I find, and the dense bush intermingled with plants of the nettle kind would allow of no closer investigation.

Best preserved of all is the outer wall of an erection of rounded form, situated in the plain and about 150 yards in diameter. It is at a distance of about 600 yards from the mountain, and was probably connected with it by means of great outworks, as appears to be indicated by the mounds of rubbish remaining. This oval has had but one entrance, which is three feet in width and five feet high and upon the northern side, that is, facing the mountain. It had, however, been at one time built up, although subsequently in part fallen in again. The cause of this was probably the brittleness of the wooden crossbeams, which had too great a weight to carry. In addition to this there are now two openings caused by crumbling of the walls. Inside, everything excepting a tower nearly thirty feet in height and in perfect preservation is fallen to ruin, but this at least can be made out that the narrow passages are disposed in the form of a labyrinth. This tower consists of similar blocks of hewn granite, and is cylindrical to a height of ten feet, then upwards to the top conical in form. At the foot its diameter is fifteen feet, at the top eight feet, and it shows no trace of any entrance. It stands between the outer wall and another close to and parallel with it, the latter having had a narrow entrance. This entrance has up to the height of a man four double layers of quite black stone, alternating with double tiers of granite. The outer walls show an attempt at ornamenting the granite—it represents a double line of zigzags between horizontal bands. This ornament is twenty feet from the ground and is employed upon a third part of the south wall on each side of the tower, and only on the outside. Everywhere else there are only rubbish, fragments, and dense bush. Some great trees three feet in diameter lift their leafy canopies to nearly twice the height of those walls which are still preserved, and many trees of vigorous growth have enclosed the blocks within their own substance. From this we may infer something as to the age of the Ruins: namely, that the Portuguese, who had no fortified trading station here before the sixteenth century, must have found these buildings already in existence.

And now a few words about the neighbourhood in which I have to spend the rainy season. It is truly lovely; well watered, fruitful, and more than 4,000 feet in actual elevation. Below my straw hut a vigorous little stream of water flows down from the projecting granite into the valley where rice is cultivated. Shady trees and constant breezes moderate the heat: rice, ground-nuts, and corn are cultivated; sheep, goats and cattle thrive well. A glorious view into the broad valley of the Tokwe extends from south-west to north-west. I regard this country as really a favourable one; the population is not hostile towards whites, is active and industrious, but suffers from two chief evils—the most blind superstition and a predilection for poisoning.

* * * * * *

Very shortly after these lines were penned, the devoted and self-sacrificing explorer's life ended. But not before he had succeeded in winning the respect and esteem of all South Africa, and in establishing, beyond a shadow of doubt, the wonderful auriferous wealth of the section of the country explored by him.

CHAPTER XIII.

Baines and his Labours—Hunting Adventures in Matabeleland.

HILE Carl Mauch was toiling and triumphing in the eastern part of the continent, Thomas Baines, F.R.G.S., another equally gallant pioneer was hard at work further inland, in the dominions of Lo Bengula, King of the Matabelies. No work on the gold regions of Africa would be complete without a reference to his labours and his life. He has done more than any other explorer, past or present, to establish the reputation of Africa as a gold land, while by his firm disposition, indomitable courage and steadiness of purpose, he endeared himself to his personal friends, amongst whom I am proud to range myself, as well as having earned the respect of all the African potentates and tribes with whom he had dealings. To this day his name, which is now a household word, is referred to with love; and sorrow is universally expressed at his untimely death, which occurred in Durban, on the 8th of May, 1875. His latest work, entitled *The Gold Regions of South-East Africa*, is one of the most reliable of guides, while his labours and example have left on the minds of the natives an influence for good that will not soon be forgotten. In his death Africa lost one of her bravest champions, and science added another name to her roll of martyrs. Without encroaching on the above-mentioned book, I may say that, while in Matabeleland, he earned the goodwill and confidence of the natives, and succeeded in obtaining a mining concession from the king; but, owing to the half-hearted support of the company which he represented, the

right fell through by lapse of time, much to the regret of Lo Bengula and his councillors.

The following letter from his able and vivid pen will serve to convey something of his labours, and while revealing some of the features of Matabeleland will, at the same time, give a faint idea of what African travel and African life is:—

"The King has given me the country, with all facilities and privileges necessary for gold working; but carefully reserving to himself the territorial right, and I have as carefully explained to him that I do not wish to impair this right, but that, on whatever terms he allows me to occupy land, he will still remain king of it, and I shall look to him for protection. My privileges extend from the Gwailo to the Ganyana Rivers, and during the past year (1870) I have done considerable exploring within those limits, and have found extensive reefs and ancient workings. These—and, indeed, our whole track from Potchefstroom—I have mapped as carefully as my opportunities would allow, by compass courses, trochiameter distance, and stellar latitudes—the latter specially cool work when the stars serve from 12 till 2, and the thermometer is below 30°—in April or May. The map is ¼-inch to a mile, and I intend to give a copy to the Surveyor's Department here for public use.

"You know, of course, that one of the chief objects of our company is to secure to Natal as large a share as possible in the advantages of the Gold Fields, and now that the affairs of Matabeleland are satisfactorily settled, I trust that this will soon begin to be accomplished. The King, Lo Bengula, is well disposed to white men, and is fully alive to the advantages to be derived from their visits to his country. Some of the regulations he enforces may at present seem rather hard and arbitrary; but I believe, as the confidence and friendship between him and the white man increases, and especially when he gets over the fear that was at first entertained, that the gold-seekers wanted to deprive him of his country, many of these will be relaxed, and made much easier to us. It must be remembered that the search for gold is a new thing to the Matabele. They were naturally suspicious of men whose object they did not understand, and they watched most narrowly every movement of the first adventurers. Even our staunch friend 'Oude Baas' (Hartley, a noted elephant hunter), did not dare to assist us until he was assured by our Matabele guide that I had in due form obtained the sanction of Um-Nombati, the head of the nation, during the interregnum, to explore the country for gold. Our success was in a great measure due to Mr. Hartley's personal knowledge of my name as an artist and traveller. I first made his personal acquaintance when he went up in 1869. He had believed me dead, but, being convinced of his error, at once offered to pilot us up to Matabeleland. I visited Matjen but declined to pay tribute, as not intending to work in his district; and passing Tati, Mr. Hartley introduced me to Mr. Lee, who held a farm and hunting-ground, by grant, from the late Moselekatzie. I showed him an introductory letter from His Excellency the Governor of Natal, and from that moment Mr. Lee took up our cause. He said he had often told Moselekatzie that when the Government sent a message respecting the Gold Fields, it would be sent in openness and friendship, and he only regretted the old chief had not lived to see the fulfilment of his words. We went on to the outpost at Manyami's and Mr. Lee followed next day, and told Manyami that he must send a special messenger in to obtain leave for me to enter, and that when I did so all the chiefs must assemble to hear the Governor's letter. After several days two indunas or petty chiefs came down from UmNombati (the counsellor of the late king, with whose name I was familiar through the writings of Capt. Harris). I had a very good interpreter (W. G. Watson, of Durban), and in answer to their questions I told them I was come on friendly business in connection with the gold in the country, and had a letter from the Governor, but I would not go into details till Mr. Lee came. When he arrived he gave them a severe lecture for exceeding their duty by prying into my business instead of waiting till they had guided me to their chief, and letting me state it to him. He called Manyami; showed him the outside of the Governor's letter, with Her Majesty's name on the envelope, and the Royal arms on the seal (and also, in consequence of this, on the panels of the waggons), and explained as much as he considered they ought to know. He accompanied us about 100 miles to UmNombati's kraal, to which he insisted on going direct, and in half an hour the venerable old Regent sent for us. I had left Jewell and Watson at Kumalo, with a heavy waggon and tired oxen, and Mr. Lee, Mr. Nelson and I at once responded to the summons. We were received in a friendly, unaffected manner, and after the first greetings the old chief, who, in a bodily sense, was infirm and helpless, but in mind as vigorous as ever, adjourned to a sunny spot in the kotla or court of audience, and there Mr. Lee opened our business. He said we had been sent by a great company in London, where Queen Victoria lived, many thousand miles across the great water, to pay him a friendly visit, and to ascertain whether the report were true that there was gold in his country; and that I had also a letter from the Governor of the English in Natal, asking him to give me leave to travel, and to protect me in doing so; that I might acquire information and send it to His Excellency, so that he might be able to make laws for those who came to seek gold, if there were any, or tell them to stay away if there were not.

"The chief said he was glad to find the English the same people he had formerly known them. He had been twice sent by his king to the borders of the great water to the Governor of Capetown, and he thanked me for coming so far to bring the letter. He gave me leave to travel and explore, but requested my promise that I would not go out of his country by another way, but would come back and tell him truly what I found, so that he might know what to say to our Governor. I made him a suitable present—a musket, ammunition, and a railway rug—and next day he told me I might keep the gold I found.

"I sent down by Mr. Lee for a fresh span of young oxen, and while waiting for them received a letter written by order of some of the chiefs to the effect that UmNombati was considered imbecile; that his permission was of no avail; and that I could not be allowed to travel because they had bound themselves to let no one but Sir John Swinburne and his party do so. I rode over to the mission station at Inyati, where I found six men deputed to fetch me back. I asked the Rev. Mr. Thomas to interpret for me, and told them that having received permission from their great chief (UmNombati), I should not pay him so poor a compliment as to ask anyone else, but should hold the liberty he gave me valid till he himself recalled it.

"Jewell brought up the new cattle, and Nelson and I went in with one waggon, having made the old chief a parting present of a warm coat, and received from him a guide named Inyassi.

"My time was entirely occupied in looking after the waggon and the route, in sketching, making geographical observations, collecting botanical specimens, and hunting for food, and Nelson's in prospecting the country. He found several reefs on either side of our path, and broke out occasional specimens with gold in them—sometimes visible to the naked eye and sometimes microscopic. In one place I believe he found alluvial gold, but it was infinitesimal. I constantly walked ahead with the guide, hunting on either side of the road. One day I broke the leg of a wildebeeste at 400 or 500 yards, and chased him for a long distance. Inyassi asked for my rifle, as he could get nearer than I could; but he could not shoot, and I had to take it in hand again, and was well tired before I got a chance to bring the animal down. Another day I fell in with a herd of buffaloes, and got near enough for a good shot, but they looked so much like our span of black oxen that I felt great compunction in firing. I killed a fine cow and wounded some others, one of which turned out of the herd and took refuge among the nopanie trees and low bushes.

I crept within forty yards, but could only see a portion of its black body without being able to distinguish the form. I fired as near as I could to the shoulder, and the creature, bleeding from mouth and nostril, rushed straight at me—with gory muzzle, flashing eyes, and sharp, black, polished horns. I was close enough to distinguish the malignant expression of every feature. One glance satisfied me. I turned at full speed, and swung myself round a clump of nopanies on the left, while Inyassi did the same on the right, letting the buffalo go straight as an arrow between us. Nelson came up, on horseback, but the buffalo had got clean away, and could not be found again. Shortly after, Nelson found a lioness sleeping on the sands, and after I had sketched her, we put two bullets into her shoulder. She reared, and sat on her haunches looking at us, her white teeth showing and her white chest also forming a capital mark—but though my Wilson rifle loads very quickly, I could not succeed in getting ready in time, and she fell into the reeds.

"We searched in every direction, sometimes skirting the edge of the reeds, sometimes climbing overhanging trees from which we could look down upon them, sometimes crossing the river to get a view from the other bank, but though the dogs —little Jack especially—did their work gallantly, we could not find her again. We made the boys fire shots whenever we thought there was a chance, standing ready, if there was any advantage, to follow it up with our rifles. But they were afraid to come even in line with us, armed only with the miserable tools miscalled firearms, which sometimes—' when much enforced, gave a hasty spark, and—straight were cold again ;' but more frequently did not give a spark at all, to say nothing of a discharge, and I rather wished I had the manufacturer or the purchaser of them on the spot to make them shoot a lion with the weapon they had provided for us.

"Finding this getting tedious, I went in, sometimes followed and sometimes preceded by an impudent little fellow named Maatchaan (a small stone, or as we might translate it, a little brick), and beating through every pathway in the long, over-arching reeds and grass, we at length came to a clump from which the dogs seemed to be driven, a low growl being just audible among their angry voices. I urged them in again, and this time the deep bass of the lion's growl was solemnly heard as they scattered out with confused yelps. I fell back two or three steps to the line formed by the people, and Nelson, who was on higher ground than I, saw a lioness (which he considered not to be the same) retreating from the other side of

Lions.

the reeds. We followed for some time in vain, and making a circuit round the country came suddenly on a rhinoceros in the long grass. I put a bullet into his shoulder, and as he turned, repeated the dose. He made off at once, and young Maatchaan, armed with my stocked Colt's revolver, gave chase at a speed which soon left us far behind, firing the miniature pellets into the neck or shoulder of the immense beast.

"I took my horse (kept only for great emergencies) and rode

on in front between thirty and forty miles, till I overtook Mr. Hartley and the other hunters at the Imbeela River, and from this time we again had the benefit of his local knowledge in pointing out where reefs or quartzose country were likely to be found. We went on to the Ganyana river, in 17° 45′ S., our furthest waggon camp, and from this I rode about thirty five miles N.W., to the kraal of a Mashona chief, named Maghoonda; he keeps three or four cattle, but is on the border of the fly country, and dare not let them go in that direction. He gave me, as usual among the Mashonas, a bowl of maasa (sour milk mixed with thick paste from Kafir cornmeal), and a little dish of meat boiled in a little water, forming soup or gravy to the maasa, and then (according to the statement of my guide) they discussed the propriety of sending me to a better world before my time, but at length concluded that it was safer to let me enjoy the present.

"It is the custom of the Mashonas to claim from the Portuguese and half-caste hunters, the tusk that touches the ground of every elephant they shoot. I had told Dr. Livingstone, ten years ago, that Englishmen would not submit to this, and now the question was settled. It never came to the English at all, but was proposed to their Matabele servants who rejected it with scorn—'Our master and king, the great Umdelagasi, never took a tusk from an English hunter, and shall you Mashonas, who are only our dogs, dare to attempt that which he refrained from?' They took me three or four miles north-east to a quartzose valley, in which were several holes from three to six feet wide, and from three to ten feet deep, but said they had forgotten what sort of metal used to be extracted. A Mashona jumped down into one, and picked me two or three pieces of quartz, and I wondered whether his ancestors had ever done the same for King Solomon, and furnished material for tales of geni and demons for the Koran and the Arabian Nights. In returning, I saw other extensive diggings. Mr. Hartley told me of more, and Nelson went prospecting daily, coming once upon a full-maned lion feeding on a dead elephant, of which I made a sketch from his description for the *Illustrated London News*.

"Our camp was broken up, and we reached the Sarua or Salagazaan River, named to commemorate the exploit of killing a little old woman. There we were met by a party of warriors, of whom half-a-dozen with white shields stood out to the front to show that they were friends. They brought a letter requesting one of the hunters to come to Inyati to explain some annoyance which had been experienced in the Transvaal by messengers who had been sent to look for Kuruman, a missing Prince of the nation. We were told verbally that all white men would have to come out of the country. We answered that they could see we were on our way, and they then went on to combine business with pleasure by doing a little marauding among the Mashonas further north, where I believe they killed seventy men and women, and took a few cattle.

"We crossed a small rivulet called the Simbo, a tributary of the Umvuli, where we broke our disselboom (pole). Having repaired this, Mr. Hartley showed me an extensive reef with old workings, and persuaded his head man, Inyoka (the serpent), to take me over the old diggings. In many of these were large thorn trees eight inches thick, showing that they must have been abandoned forty or fifty years ago, but not proving for them a high antiquity. I suppose they were worked by the Mashonas when the Portuguese colonies on the Zambezi were prosperous, and the gold either carried to those settlements or sold to traders visiting or residing more or less permanently among the native tribes—in fact, Mr. Hartley found the ruins of a house between Imbecla and Umvuli, and an old man in his service says a white man lived there in his father's time. Mr. Nelson, my mineralogist, was away prospecting at this time, but after his return he examined this reef, and advised me to take possession of it in presence of our guide; and we did so, naming the granite kopjies near it 'Hartley's Hills.' Three good stellar observations subsequently taken placed this in 18° 11′ 39″. Sir John

Swinburne had built a hut and sunk a couple of shafts about seven furlongs south, on the Umvuli.

"We again received a summons to come out of the country, and as we toiled on with our weary oxen the army overtook us. We had killed an eland, and gave over to them what meat we could spare; and when we got into difficulties in the UmNyati River, Setlaasi, the chief who—except in professional matters, such as killing Mashonas, &c.—was a very good-hearted fellow, set his men to help us through. The oxen were outspanned, and 150 warriors, laying down their arms, manned the trek-tow, and after a little cargo had been discharged, succeeded in starting the waggon, and hauled her out with a run, chanting the while in unison. They had an intense desire to taste coffee and sugar, so I made them a great brew, and kept kettles of hot water ready. Setlaas and I had the first cup, then he diluted it and served it to his officers and men—the latter getting it warm, but exceedingly pure. However, we sweetened it a little as it went round, and afterwards I gave strips of calico for head bands to the men—150 in number.

"Reaching Inyati, I rode to UmNombati, the chief and regent of the country, who had removed to Inthlathlangelo, and I found I had been accused of having dug the holes, which in reality had been dug by Sir John Swinburne, but several native friends had given evidence in my favour, and now my guide added his testimony, and I was completely cleared. I was requested to go out of the country while the successor to Umzelegasi was being chosen, but I was also told that if I only went a little past Inthlathlangela they would be satisfied, as they were too friendly to me to drive me much further. However, I had to go to Tati for supplies, and spent the summer on Mr. Lee's farm, meanwhile making a visit of friendship to Lo Bengula, who had been requested to accept the dignity of king. He refused for a long time and made every effort to find his elder brother Kuruman, but at length evidence, satisfactory to the nation, was brought forward that Kuruman had been killed at Thaba Induna, and Lo Bengulu accepted the offer, and was installed in the dignity and power of his late father—10,000 warriors being present at the ceremonial, while 1,500 remained disaffected. Mr. Lee was invited to be there, and was asked whether he accepted Lo Bengulu as his king; he said he coincided in the choice of the nation, and was told that the grants made to him by Umselegasi were confirmed. He brought forward the affairs of the company, and the king told him, 'Yes, Mr. Baines can have the northern gold fields.'

"In April, I started from Mr. Lee's place, and reached the king's new town of Gibbe klaik, where he received me in the most friendly manner, and desired me to make my request. I asked for the country between Gwailyo and Ganyany rivers, and he gave me liberty to go in and explore and dig for gold; to erect houses or machinery; to use the roads and exercise all privileges necessary for that object; telling me that all details were my business, and included in his general grant. He asked particularly after Mr. Nelson, who had gone down to Natal to lay the specimens, &c., before Mr. Behrens, the agent of our company, and to convey information to His Excellency, the Governor, and requested me to remain a few days and go down with him to a new kraal on the Limpopo side of the water-shed, in a warmer situation than the bleak site of Gibbe klaik.

"We were happy to receive the new missionary, Mr. Thompson, who at the king's request held service in my tent on Sunday—Mr. Watson interpreting, which he does very fluently, and reading from the English scripture, translating (or rather reading it into Zulu) as he goes on. Mrs. Thompson also became a great favourite with the king's wives and sisters.

"Of course, we had to give presents. Mine was a salted hunting horse, valued at £75, though by paying in beads I bought him for a trifle less—a saddle, bridle, and rifle, making it up to £100. This was our entrance fee, besides blankets, beads, clothing, &c., occasionally.

"We went on to Inyati, and thence to Emampangene to buy

goats and corn. We were nearly a week going thirty-five miles—the waggon axles even sinking into the swampy ground. We actually ploughed up with the wheel a great burrowing frog that thought himself perfectly safe till next season, but when he came to the surface, we cooked and ate him, like a chicken.

"Watson was a great adept at setting spring guns for wolves, *i.e.*, hyænas and jackals. He digs a hole in the ground so that the creature has to put his head in for the bait, and in tugging at it he discharges a gun which shoots him through the head. Sometimes he gets away, but generally wounded, and it is to be hoped the sudden alarm bears fruit to repentance and makes him a sadder and a wiser wolf. Other things are taken with snares and springs—even an eagle (a Bateleur) was caught one night thus. At Emampangene we saw a man who professed to be 'the Son of God' (as Watson translated it), who exhibited wondrous feats of strength and endurance—the principal of which was dancing, or rather jumping, by the action of the ankles and muscles of the foot alone, keeping all the rest of the body rigid, and only once now and then indulging in a few *ad libitum* capers as a relief to the monotony of the performance. I believe he was in reality the son of a man who lives in a mountain not far from Inthlathlangela, and who by shouting from a cave with peculiar echoes, contrives to pass for something supernatural. It is certain that some rocks and particular places are held sacred, and the Mashonas go to them to perform some act of worship, and some of the Matabele follow their example—though to them generally, their king is their God, and they know no other. Still there seems to be some kind of religion natural or acquired among them. My cousin, Mr. Richard Watson, of Sydenham, heard a Matabeli mention God, and to try him, he asked, 'Where is he?' The reply was 'Here—all around us—everywhere—the sky is his roof and the earth is his floor.' 'But,' continued Watson, 'I do not see him.' 'No,' said the Kafir, 'but you may see his things —the oxen on the hills; the corn in the fields; the water in the rivers; and other things everywhere.' I fancy, however, such advanced views as this are rare.

"We kept along the high lands to the south of our former road, crossing the Umvungu and Gwailo about twenty miles higher up, and came into it again near the Quaequae. I generally walked ahead with the guide, sometimes finding a quartz reef, and sometimes shooting a buck. At Sebague, we turned out in force to hunt buffaloes, and in a clump of mopanies, about a mile down the river, we came upon a herd. At first, however, I only saw one, and I gave him a shot in the shoulder; this forced him to turn back into the bush, from whence another immediately came trotting out towards me. I had a Wilson breechloader, which is very quick and handy, and was ready to give him a shot in the shoulder also, but Jewell coming up to support me, delivered his fire and helped to turn them out. I now closed with the first bull, whose shoulder appeared to be broken, and after two or three shots succeeded in breaking his hind leg; leaving Jewell to despatch him, I ran on after the other shouting to the men to turn him in front. I got one shot into his ribs and then lost sight of him for a moment, but the men had headed him, and before I could get up to the chase again, they had overturned him with a broadside. Still he was not dead, although unable to rise, and his dark eyes glared upon us from under his massive horns most expressively as we gathered round. Jewell gave him an eleven to the lb. ball from his Westley Richards, under the ear, but I believe that the bullet split upon the hard bones and scattered itself, instead of penetrating to the brain. I took my sketch book from the boy who carried it, and who had orders not to run after wounded beasts nor mix with the chase to the detriment of aforesaid book, which orders, of course, he always forgot in the excitement of the fray, and being anxious that Jewell should get a photograph I sent for the trek oxen to haul the carcases home. The second was a fine old bull, with a splendid pair of horns—the first a young one.

"I also observed the latitude of our camp, and marked it on a tree. I have done this in several places in order to make definite points of departure. We remained some days here and made a trek tow out of the hides. Watson shot some wolves, and we turned out at night to shoot a lion, but though he only retreated slowly, he would not give us battle and we could not by any means get sight of him for a fair shot.

"We crossed the Bembesi, called Bembesi-enia, or the 'other Bembesi,' to distinguish it from one of the same name at Zwong Endaba; here also I found quartz reefs and hills with the ruins of the stone kraals and huts of the Mashonas upon their summits, the inhabitants having been massacred by the Matabele in former years; then again we crossed the Umnyati (or Buffalo) with its castellated granite hills around the drift; the Umgesi, so named from a famous Mashona chief Umgesa, who governed the country from Umnyati to Umvuli; and the Umgesana, or little Umgesi, sometimes called Umgwasaan, from a word signifying to stab —but I believe the former to be the correct name. Next came the Umzweswie, a very picturesque little stream, the drift overshadowed with tall trees, amid which the spreading soft wooded pao pisa (of the Portuguese), mosaawe (of the natives), or *Kigelia pinnata*, with its long inedible fruit like great polonies or cucumbers pendant from cord-like stalks three feet long, while near it grows a kind of strychnia called the Kafir orange, bearing a hard-shelled fruit filled with seeds embedded in a pleasant orange-like pulp; then turning to the left and north out of the hunter's road, we crossed the Umvuli, at Kigelia drift. The natives, who now seemed to think the acquisition of a pretty pebble a certain means of getting a pipe of tobacco, picked up several bits of quartz, agate and coarse jasper. We passed the unfortunate holes 'dug in the king's country when there was no king to give permission,' and reached our first location at Hartley Hills. I made a trip about twelve miles down the river, and saw several reefs, but did not succeed in killing anything, and at once set about erecting a house for the accommodation of Mr. Nelson and the workmen I expected him to bring up from Natal. My plan was two rooms of fourteen feet square, and ten feet high to the wall plate, a six-foot passage between, and pitched roof to give plenty of air and room in case any one should be attacked by fever. We went round the forest and selected mopanie poles, which Watson, with a gang of Matabeli cut down, while Jewell and I saw to the digging of the holes to insert them, and in a few days we had the satisfaction of seeing the walls in frame, the gables and ridge poles, and some of the principal rafters in place—not forgetting a tall straight pole in an open space in front, from which the Union Jack floated daily.

"While we were thus at work, one morning, we heard heavy guns at a distance, and our friends Molony and Leask arrived on horseback about noon. We went to greet them, but all our cheerful hopes were dashed, as by a thunderstroke, by the news that not less than seven of their party were dead of fever, and nearly all were more or less affected, Molony himself being ill, and Leask almost the only one in tolerable health. Mr. George Wood had lost his wife and his child; Mr. Jebbe, a talented German explorer, was dead, having previously, in his delirium, destroyed his papers. Mr. McDonald, Toris (a half-caste waggon-driver), and poor Willie Hartley—a gallant young hunter, who bade fair to rival the fame of his well-known father—had also succumbed. They invited me to visit their camp, nine or ten miles to the S.E., and next morning I set out on foot, Mr. Wood kindly sending a horse to meet me. It was a sorrowful sight to witness the weakness, both of body and mind, left by the fever among so many dashing hunters, whom I had known but a few months before in the full pride of health and strength, ready for chase or battle with any beast, no matter how fierce, how swift, or cunning. It was almost impossible for me to gather the details of the fatal season with anything like correctness, because their memory had been so disturbed, that they could not give me a consecutive account, and, of course, I did not like to press them on so painful a subject.

"George Wood returned with me next day to Hartley's Hill, and all the waggons were afterwards brought on, crossing the Simbo River and camping at Constitution Hill, about a mile north of us—the latter name being because Mr. Leask, who gained the brevet rank of doctor, made the invalids walk to the hill once a day. Those who could rode out now and then, and began to shoot game as they gained strength; but we subsequently heard that Mr. McGillewie, with Jennings' party, and Mr. Saunders, remained ill for a long time.

"Jewell and I took my waggon, and one belonging to poor Willie, and went south-east, crossing the Zinlundasi, and the sources of Umzweswie, Umgesi and Umnyati rivers, and then passing over the Watershed, 4,700 feet high, as nearly as I remember, or perhaps 4,470. On the way we enjoyed a fine view of the mountain called Inthaba-wahella, and the plains beyond and below us, then descending by small spruits, running to the Saabi or Sabea River, we crossed the Kitoro, also one of its tributaries, and winding among granite hills, with Mashona villages perched on them in almost inaccessible situations, where they had been placed for fear of the Matabele, we came to the village of Umtigesi, whence men came out to guide us to the plateau about half-way up the hill, we outspanned not very far from the grass and pole house formerly occupied by George Wood. The people came readily and unsuspectingly out to meet us from all the villages, but had Matabele been seen not accompanying English waggons, they would have run like the coveys of their own hills to the securest shelter.

"We could not open the market for a long time because Mr. Wood had bought largely, and having satisfied their present demand for beads, they had enhanced the price; and it was not until evening that I bought the chief's goats for supper thereby fixing the price and opening the traffic.

"I got a good observation at night, and I think the latitude was 18° 47'. The next day was a busy one, large crowds came with corn, but goods were sparingly bought, and pack oxen only promised. Umtigasi came himself, and generally sat with me to see that his people kept order, while Jewell and the people purchased corn, but sometimes the chief would mount on the waggon-seat, and, flourishing a sjambok over his unruly followers, drive the idle and disorderly to a distance.

"The Mashona men wear their hair long, just as you see it on the old Egyptian monuments. They tie little tufts of their crisp wool up in bandages of red bark till they look like the cockscombs of our own clowns, each of these tufts they saturate with the oil of the ground-nut or Mashambana till they force the ringlets to a length of nine or ten inches, or even a foot. These are parted in the middle, put back over the ears, and confined by a snood, giving an effeminate look to the features. Grease and charcoal are liberally applied, and the dandies carry a small pillow (or rather a three or four-legged stool) on which, when they sleep, they lay their necks to keep their well-oiled heads high off the ground. They remind me very much of the Damaras, on the West Coast, only that the Damaras use red clay instead of charcoal.

"The Mashonas are clever smiths. They seem to keep a supply of smelted iron at the mountain Wahella already mentioned (which is also called Coedza, the giraffe). This they bring to their smithy, and, raising a sufficient heat in a charcoal fire by means of a clever pair of goat-skin bellows, the smith picks the metal out with a green withy, and laying it down on a flat stone, makes his 'hammerman' deliver heavy blows with another stone, weighing, perhaps, 50 lbs., and then he follows up his work with an iron hammer of 3 lbs. to 6 lbs. *with a handle*—a most unusual thing among savages. Hoes, axes, assegais, barbed and bearded in the most cruelly-ingenious manner, arrow heads, and keys for musical instruments, as well as walking-sticks, rings, beads, and personal ornaments, are made very neatly. Wire is drawn by forcing the small end of a bar into a hole formed by two grooves made in the faces of two blocks of iron, placed face to face in a hole in a stout tree, and wedged closely into contact. A lever is used to draw the iron through, and the blocks are then wedged more and more closely to reduce it, and when necessary blocks with smaller grooves are substituted.

"Their cassansas or musical instruments, consisting of a number of iron springs arranged on a hollow key-board as big as a quarto volume, and tinkled with the thumb-nails, are very ingenious and well-arranged. They have a regular scale; I can play part of 'God save the Queen,' on them, but cannot get through the whole of it. They have various recognised tunes, which are very popular, and I have known Portuguese on the Zambezi who can play them most melodiously. The sound is increased by enclosing the key-board in a calabash hung round with loose discs of shell, which jingle slightly.

"The Mashona pack oxen are trained to carry burdens laid upon their backs without being girthed. When they are offered for sale, a huge sack of Mashambana nuts like a great mattress, bulky but light, is laid on them, and they are required, without being led, to walk up to the purchaser without throwing the pack off.

"We returned to Hartley's Hill, where we found Watson had shot a crocodile—a very bold act, as the Matabele suspect that a man doing so intends to use the liver for witchcraft against the lives of his neighbours. I had great difficulty in persuading the Kafirs to haul it ashore, though I went into the water myself to make the line fast. Jewell and I travelled twenty-two miles down the Umvuli to the N.W., where I shot a waterbok and wild pig, and we saw some 'seacows,' but they were so wild we could not approach them. We saw several reefs and old workings, and ruins of Mashona villages. Some of these I named 'Waterbok Reef,' 'Jewell Reef,' and 'Mackenzie Reef.'

"Mr. Hartley arrived at our house some time after, and was

greatly affected on hearing of the loss of his son. I was also much disappointed at finding that our mineralogist (Mr. Nelson) had not returned, and that I should have to take upon myself his work without having his skill to qualify me for it.

"Mr. Leask offered to guide us to Willie's grave, and we set out one morning, I having my sketch-book and Jewell his photographic camera; but we came across elephants' spoor on the way, and Mr. Hartley—sacrificing his private feelings to the welfare of his fellow-hunters—gave the word to follow. They took us eleven miles up the Umvuli, then crossed to the south, and passed within a mile of Willie's grave; it was a hard trial for the father to pass the spot where his dead son lay; but he pressed bravely on, and after twenty-five miles of travelling we caught sight of the elephants. Hartley shot two, and Molony, Leask, and Giffard one each. Subsequently we went out again and found the grave, about twelve miles E.S.E. of Hartley's Hill. After Mr. Hartley had been left a little space alone beside it, I made a sketch and Jewell photographed it. There was no stone there, and only a heap of bushes were laid over the mound, while the initials 'W. J. H. 19/5/71,' were cut on one of the trees above it. I am afraid that when a few years of grass fires shall have passed over the spot, there will be no sign of the brave young hunter's resting-place.

"Afterwards Mr. Hartley took me about twenty miles N.N.W. to see the ruins of a Portuguese house he had found, and which had been inhabited about forty or fifty years ago. We saw very extensive reefs and old workings, but next morning, while we were looking for the house, we came on elephants' spoor again and turned away to track it. Presently, a piece of grass kicked forward indicated the fact that the elephants had begun to run, so we galloped on through bush and brier in hot haste, but they had gone into the 'fly country,' and we dared not follow them. We saw more reefs and workings as we returned to camp.

"I spent several days in digging about three feet deep in our reef at Hartley's Hill, and with Mr. Hartley's assistance found several specks of gold in stones which I have preserved. Mr. Hartley also very kindly sent his head man Inyoka and the same Mashona who had guided Herr Mauch, and showed me several other workings. Then Mr. George Wood arrived, and invited me to his camp, very near Maghoonda's village, where I was in 1869, and showed me where the Mashonas, no doubt incited by the inquiries I had then made, had resumed their ancient industry, and had commenced picking out quartz, laying it in piles with dry branches alternately and firing it; then, when sufficiently burned, crushing it on a stone with a round pebble, as the Hottentots grind coffee or a painter does colours, and afterwards washing the grains of gold out. He gave me some of this in a quill which he had bought from them. I am preserving it as a valuable evidence, for if they with their imperfect means can get gold, what can we do with proper appliances? We also saw extensive reefs, both in going and returning.

"As Mr. Hartley had commenced his homeward bound trip, I broke up our establishment and followed. We shot a sea cow on the Umgesi, and at Umnyati I cut a specimen of the bark of the baobab, which is said to be as good as quinine, in cases of fever. I have sent it to Dr. J. D. Hooker, at the Royal Botanic Gardens, Kew, to be tested.

"We went out again on the spoor of elephants, and came across the edge of the shales and slates, but I cannot say much about gold quartz, for we came in sight of a herd of about 150 elephant cows and calves, and another of about 40 bulls. It had been agreed that the whole herd should be driven till it was weary, and then the hunters should kill all they could, but the rule was soon broken. It was a magnificent sight. I had the pleasure of being in at the death of seven out of eight that were killed, and of being chased by one. Mr. Hartley's Mashona took me to some rich reefs and workings down the Bembesi and Sebaque rivers, but I shot a rhinoceros, a buffalo and two pigs, and the people lived so well they made a conspiracy to go no further, and concealed their knowledge of reefs further on. However, I can find them for myself when I want them.

"At Inyati we were most hospitably received by the Revs. Sykes and Thompson, and their wives—the latter had actually grown a crop of English wheat during his first year's mission. He accompanied us to the king's village. Mr. Hartley and I went to see the spot he had chosen for a mission station, to be called Hope Fountain. I am happy to say my agent, Mr. Lee, was mainly instrumental in procuring the grant of it from the king, who now for the first time has the principles of a Christian mission society explained to him. Inyati was given to Moffat, and the missionaries there are called Moffat's children; but the ground here, however, is given to the London Society to hold as long as they use it for mission purposes—when they cease to do so it reverts to the king. Mr. Thompson seems to be in favour with the white men here, and he is right in cultivating their friendship, for if he can improve the standard of morality among them, he will be doing good work for them and the natives they live among. Every man responded to his invitation to service, and we had eighteen or twenty each Sunday in my tent. The grand old psalm tune, sung by so many powerful voices, brought the Kafirs far and near to listen. Some of them I think expected we were going to get up a war dance. In the native services Watson read to the Matabele, and I to those who understood Dutch, Mr. Thompson conducting the service in English. By our aid the people were fairly attentive.

"The king has been greatly occupied with business lately; two large marauding parties having returned with about 8,000 head of cattle, and the reviews and dances, and distribution of cattle, occupied several days. About 100 to 200 Mashonas, men, women, and children, have been killed, yet the king, though sanctioning all this, considers he is doing no wrong. He is a good natured fellow, takes great interest in my sketching, and takes kindly notice of Lee's little boys. The other day he gave his army a bull to eat alive to show their ferocity; they had got it down and were cutting its shoulder out when it escaped, and after nearly killing Mr. Grant, it gored one of my horses (value £45), which died in two days.

"The king has made me an unofficial visit, and I showed him a bag of quartz, pulling out a single piece in which a speck of gold was visible. Mr. Lee explained how little gold there was to so much stone, and how great was the labour of extracting it.

"Mr. Lee asked if he were fully satisfied with the manner in which I had acted on the privilege he had given me, and he said yes, he was perfectly satisfied, and would not withdraw his favour till I should myself do something wrong to forfeit it; in fact, Mr. Lee assured me that so far as the king's favour was concerned, I was perfectly safe.

"On the day when he came officially, the king asked whether I had found gold. I answered in the affirmative, and he formally renewed the privilege he had already given me to dig for gold, guarding only against my setting up any claim that would deprive him of his territorial rights, which, of course, I do not want to injure. I told him I should look upon him as king of the country, and as my protector in it. In return he gave me the gold of the country, and the privilege of working it freely, but he would not bargain for a price lest it should seem like conveying away his claim to the sovereignty of his country. I thanked him, and told him I would each year make him such a present as I thought he would be pleased with (this I expect will be a salted horse, saddle and bridle, and a rifle, to the value of £100). We managed to get up a couple of dinners, the first by Mr. Kisch, the second by Mr. Hartley and myself, and invited the king and his sister, who were highly pleased. We even mustered wine enough (thanks to Mr. Carter) to drink toasts with, and had songs *ad libitum*.

"I suppose you have heard that the Portuguese Governor from Quillimaine has constituted himself and other officers a diplomatic deputation to the Transvaal for the purpose of settling their respective boundaries. Indeed it is high time, for the Transvaal on paper claims Matabeleland as far north as the Changani River, and Portugal claims down to the 26th degree of south latitude ; so that we are like Sir Boyle Roche's bird in three countries at once, only as neither the Transvaal Government nor His Excellency of Quillimaine dare send a representative to assert their claims, and the Matabele are all we have to deal with.

Now that we are opening the gold-fields, His Excellency thinks he may as well furbish up an old cession by the Emperor of Monomotapa, 300 years ago, and he writes me a letter to tell me that as I am in the district of Sofala, in the province of Mozambique, I cannot explore without permission of the King of Portugal. I have answered that I am not in the province of Sofala, but in the country of the Mashonas, conquered by Umzelegazi, and given to me by his son Lo Bengulu, and that my duty is to go on working, leaving the question of boundaries to the Governments of our respective countries.

"On reaching Potchefstroom I met his Excellency and saw the published map on which he relies, and on this I showed him that the country occupied by me on account of our company, is not in the district of Sofala, nor in Senna, nor in Tette, but is marked there with the tribal name, Mashonas : Mozambique is far away to the north of Tette, and we are perfectly clear of the Portuguese country, unless his Excellency should be allowed to stretch his claims as far as he likes, and draw a red and blue line over the map of Africa. He told me they had 3,000 fighting men at Tette, and they were going to extend the district to Ganyana. I said, 'Well, we will not quarrel; Ganyana is my northern boundary.' 'Then,' said he, 'we will extend it to Umnyati.' I told him the Matabele were a warlike people, and would probably fight. He said they did not wish to fight if they could help it, but would convince Lo Bengulu by diplomacy. I told him if he could convince Lo Bengulu, by diplomacy, that his country did not belong to him, he would do more than I considered likely. He said the Emperor of Monomotapa had ceded all the country as far as the Hottentots, 300 years ago, and it belonged to the Portuguese by right of conquest. In reply, I said the Portuguese had never occupied the country in such a manner as to give them a right to it, and the few solitary traders who had gone in, had abandoned it fifty years ago, and it was now, in fact, derelict. Beside which, if he relied on right of conquest, Umzelegaze had conquered it, and Lo Bengulu who held it in his father's right, had given it to me, and, further, I thought a living Lo Bengulu better than a dead Monomotapa. I find that the Chevalier Duprat does not coincide with these claims, which are so easy to extend on paper; he considers that the Portuguese line runs from the coast up the river Doro, to the foot of the Drakensberg, thence along the foot of the Berg to where the Limpopo breaks through and thence in a straight line to Zumbo. This last is only an imaginary line named almost at random, because little was known of the natural boundaries.

"I think, however, that the frontiers as laid down on the map previously referred to, could most conveniently be retained, *i.e.*, Sofala on the east of the continuation of the Drakensberg, Senna on the north of this last, and Tette on the north of a spur which seems to turn westward and send several small tributaries down to the Zambesi; the land granted to us lying on the west of the Drakensberg or coast range, and on the south of the mountains last named. There is one ray of comfort, however: I believe his Excellency does not intend to do more than protest, and I have no wish to interfere with this amusement, so long as it pleases him and does not hurt me."

ELANDS SPRUIT. Road to Barberton.

(From a Photograph by Robert Harris.)

CHAPTER XIV.

THE GOLD FIELDS OF TO-DAY.—BARBERTON.

DESPITE the labours of Mauch and Baines, and the reports of others, such as Mohr, Hübner, Elton—together with my own notes which were published from time to time in the Colonial papers—the bulk of the settlers in South Africa refused to either believe in, or seek for, the hidden treasures of the wilderness. Such being the case, it is not to be wondered at that the outside world took but little heed of the oft-repeated announcements of new gold discoveries. This apathy on the part of the colonists was to be traced, in the first place, to poverty and inability to go afield, and in the second, to the almost ceaseless war scares. In 1879, the grim reality burst on the country, in the invasion and conquest of Zululand by Imperial forces. Close following this came the Transvaal war of independence; and after that came, as a natural consequence, a trade depression of terrible severity. Confidence was destroyed, and distrust reigned between Boers, Blacks, and British. Zululand, despite the so-called "settlement," was in a disturbed state, the Transvaal was crippled, and Natal nerveless and hopeless. But the very severity of the stagnation proved its cure, for men were driven in sheer despair to seek for some means of earning a livelihood. So shouldering their packs, they started off northward and westward. Very soon the results of their explorations became apparent. Finds in bewildering number were announced in all directions, and a wave of enthusiasm swept over the country. Farmers left their ploughs, clerks their desks, clergymen their flocks, and husbands their wives. "Gold! gold! gold!" was the cry of the streets, of the market places, of the firesides; tiny syndicates, with scarcely any capital, were formed and dissolved with magic rapidity. Rumours of wonderfully rich discoveries, at almost regular intervals, stimulated the excitement, while the stream of adventurers kept up, until the wilderness became no longer a lone place.

The eastern districts of the Transvaal Republic attracted the first rush, which took place in 1884-5. Alluvial gold, it was said, would be found in vast quantities in the valleys of the Kaap and Queen rivers. This hope, however, was soon swallowed up in the grander certainty of reef discoveries. The first mining camp of importance was established on lands owned by Mr. G. P. Moodie. Towards the close of 1884, over one thousand diggers—most of them inexperienced men—were assembled in this locality, and busily engaged in developing the reefs; but owing to the transfer of the property to a company, whose conditions were considered unreasonable, bitter disputes took place between the diggers and those who represented the Company. Many of the men left in disgust, and scattering in all directions, soon established the fact that the whole region was exceedingly rich in gold. At first but little capital was forthcoming, and as a result, a reaction similar to that which succeeded the war took place, but the inherent value of the region soon asserted itself, and Moodie's sank into comparative insignificance when the famous Sheba Reef came to light. Midway between the old centre, which was called Moodie's Camp, and the new discovery, the town of Barberton sprang up, and in the course of a twelve-month assumed the appearance of an old-established settlement.

Still further and further afield went the diggers, and still the news of fresh discoveries filled the newspapers, until men were bewildered by the extent of their finds and crippled by the constant outlay, for reef digging, unlike alluvial washing, requires heavy initial expenditure. The region in which this drama was enacted, may be described as lying to the eastward of the Godwaan plateau, which presents a precipitous krantz or cliff to it. One thousand five hundred or two thousand feet below the crest of this cliff lies the Valley of the Kaap, so-called from a "cape" or headland that overlooks the river. Viewed from the heights, the valley of De Kaap presents a basin of about forty by thirty miles. Rising tier upon tier, the mountain barriers, with their crests in many cases swathed in mist, carry the eye far into cloudland. Deep below, amongst volcanic cones and rocky ridges, flow the Queen and De Kaap rivers, while stray clusters of trees serve to relieve the monotony of the hills. Outcrops of white quartz or "blows," as they are locally called, occur on nearly every hillock, while the tents and houses of the gold hunters, which are to be seen nearly everywhere, impart an appearance of life and motion to the place.

The town of Barberton, which has a population of about 2,000, stands slightly to the south-east of the valley, on elevated ground. Close behind it the hills tower to still greater altitudes, and are dotted here and there with the tents or the workings of the miners. As far as I could ascertain, about 400 stamps are at work, and the output of gold is daily increasing. Hotel accommodation is good, while quarters at private boarding-houses and other lodgings are to be had at reasonable prices. There are three banks, two exchanges, a theatre, and several other places of amusement. Three newspapers are published regularly, and all the latest journals from England and the colonies are to be had. Regular mails are delivered, and the health of the town is good.

I do not consider it advisable to attempt any detailed description of the several properties and works. To do full justice to the subject would take up too much time, and answer no good purpose.

CHAPTER XV.

THE WITWATERSRANDT FIELDS.

HE district of Witwatersrandt is a most peculiar and interesting one; it is here that the, at present, most promising Gold Fields of South Africa are situated. The "White Waters Range" lies about thirty miles to the southward of Pretoria, the capital of the Transvaal, and a like distance northward of the charming little township of Heidelburg. As early as 1854, gold was said to have been found in the district, which is composed of open bleak ranges of grassy and barren-looking hills, of slight elevations; in fact, a better idea of the region would be conveyed by describing it as a rolling prairie, seamed here and there with water-courses and gullies, washed out by the summer floods.

In December, 1885, the firm of Struben Bros. having great faith in the future of the place, erected a five-stamp battery on one of their farms in the vicinity. The successful results of this and other ventures culminated in a rush in 1886.

Since then, constant discoveries have been made between Pretoria and the Vaal River, and a heavy mining population has collected. During my visit, in the latter part of 1887, the digging population of the district was estimated at about 10,000, 7,000 of which were located in and about the Witwatersrandt. The town of Johannesburg sprang up, and, although its foundations were laid in the closing months of 1885, it is now a large, prosperous and well-built centre, possessing solid buildings, established trade and

PANORAMIC VIEW OF JOHANNESBURG, No. 1

PANORAMIC VIEW OF JOHANNESBURG, No 2.

The Union Steam Ship Company, Limited.

commerce, and social institutions worthy of a borough of a hundred years.

On the occasion of my last visit I favoured the Natal route, because my starting point was Durban, the sea port of Natal. After an enjoyable railway ride of 189 miles, we arrived at Ladysmith, in the uplands of the colony, and taking seats in the post-cart, which is a commodious covered four-wheeled spring waggon, drawn by four—and sometimes six—well-fed

Post and Passenger Car to Gold Fields.

horses, set off in a westerly direction towards the frontier of the Free State. After a drive of thirty miles, during which we changed horses three times, at stations where refreshments were to be had at extremely reasonable terms, we commenced the ascent of the Drakensberg at Van Reenan's Pass, or "Poort" as it is called. Rising by steady stages to higher latitudes, we were regaled with the most bewitching scenery; but the climax was gained when, winning the summit, we turned and looked across the very scene which Piet Retief and his followers revelled in, in the old emigrant days. Instead of a lone, wild Eden of beauty, our eyes now rested on a wide stretch of meadow and hill, dotted here and there with prosperous homesteads, sheep-runs, cornfields, and orchards; here and there the long dark line of the railway track peeped out, stretching for miles upon miles over the hills, while further to the north the fresh-turned earth revealed where the labourers were hard at work, pushing on the track to the coalfields, twenty miles off. Since then, that line has been opened and the fuel resources of the Colony tapped. Close at our feet could be seen the winding and ascending road, where in a few years the railway will doubtless be cleaving its way. At the time of my visit, however, traffic had to be carried by ox-waggons of the primitive sort, and the only reminder I had that I stood in Africa, and not in England, was the long teams of toiling cattle who, in their yokes, patiently drag the lumbering waggons up the incline.

Taking a last look at Natal, we turned our faces towards the open prairies of the Free State and at an elevation of 8,000 to 10,000 feet above the sea, sped on through the dry and bracing air towards Harrismith, the frontier town of the Republic, which is as English in appearance as it is in name. Good accommodation is to be had here, at Durban—and even London—prices; luxuries such as liquors, cigars and literature, are, as I have elsewhere said, about 15 per cent. dearer than in England. Next morning betimes we started off with fresh teams and a half-caste driver, whose brawny hands had for twenty years held the ribbons and guided the destinies of the Royal Mails from one Republic to the other.

With a horizon of blue distance relieved on the eastward by the rugged crests of the Quathlamba, we sped on and on across the plain over a road which, thanks to Nature and not art, was smooth and good. Heading northwards, we drove for sixty miles or more with scarcely a sign of cultivation, saving now and again when a Boer homestead would heave in sight, with its orchards of apple and apricot trees, its green cornfields and its thickets of Australian blue gum trees.

In the open spaces, now and again, we startled a herd of wild deer, who, after gazing at us for a moment with their great black and expressive eyes, would lay back their heads and gallop off to safer and more secluded pastures. As we approached the vicinity of the Vaal River, a stray Boer, mounted on a rugged but well-bred horse, would pull up, and without removing his ever-lighted pipe from his lips, yell an uncouth but kindly salutation at me; for I was known to many of them as the "trekker," which being freely interpreted means "traveller."

The Vaal River is a deep and considerable stream, often quite impassable by reason of floods and freshets. It is provided with a floating pontoon, called a "punt," which is hauled across with a load of mules, men, and waggons, by means of a strong wire rope. On the other side stretched the same wide rolling plains, seamed here and there by a gully or spruit, into which we would splash, and if the fates were favourable, out of which we would climb mud-be-draggled but smiling. Night fell before we had gone far, and turning towards a Boer homestead we besought hospitality, and received a right-royal mead of it. As we are now on the threshold of an Africander farmer's abode, it may be well to say a few words touching this sturdy, brave, flaxen-haired, primitive but hospitable people.

Owing to the wars and other troubles, a very natural estrangement had sprung up between them and the English settlers and tourists. Another equally natural reason for the feeling, which is now, I am happy to say, dying out, is the fact that we are better educated and more polished in manners than they are, or can be expected to be. This is always a source of division in all lands. But if the tourist is a man of the world, is easy, unaffected and well-mannered, the ice soon melts and the best side of the Boer comes out. This particular Dutchman was a man of some consideration, being a field-cornet (J.P.) and landowner of considerable extent. No sooner were the horses removed from the mail-cart than he appeared in the doorway, smoking as usual. After shaking hands in a half-hearted sort of manner with us, he stood round vacantly regarding the hills, the sky, and the on-coming night. After a few admiring remarks about his fine stone-built homestead, which were sincerely meant, and a passing word of praise on his "veldt," or grazing ground, I expressed a wish to see his sheep—as the herds happened at the time to be passing.

Upon this there was a visible thawing; turning towards the pens, he in a few moments was earnestly discoursing on "scab," and other diseases and troubles, with which my acquaintanceship was distant and vague. I listened until the coming night closed the chapter, and turning, he led the way through the spacious kitchen to a lofty sitting-room, the furniture of which was of a somewhat gaudy and incongruous style; an harmonium stood in one corner, a broad table in another, and chairs and sofas were scattered about. Two tall, strapping sons (also smoking pipes) rose to receive me with a hand-shake. Three daughters of ample dimensions, four small boys, and the tall, fine-looking mother now entered, and shook hands solemnly and slowly. This over, we all sat down and kept silence until the mother invited us to supper. The meal consisted of coffee, fresh butter, brown bread (home grown and baked), venison, shot on his own ground, and stewed apples, apricots and other fruits from his orchard. Excepting the sugar, the dishes and the table cloth, everything was of home manufacture, even the table, which was of yellow wood.

After an hour or two of smoking, and a mild chat about the gold discoveries, we all retired, but not to one common bed, as many writers have stated when describing the Boers. My chamber was well appointed, and the bed (which was a feather one) was large and only too comfortable, for when our Jehu, next morning, "blew a blast upon the bugle-horn," I was loth to leave the brown, but sweet and clean sheets. Having partaken of a cup of coffee, and thanked my kindly host, hostess, and family, I jumped into the post-chaise and away we went again. That night we won our way to Heidelberg, a town which, as I have stated, lies about sixty miles south and slightly to the east of Pretoria, the capital. Here, rival hotels, conducted on English principles, keep prices reasonable, and visitors are made thoroughly comfortable and cosy.

The next day we realised that we were indeed on the "Gold Fields." Trenches and workings seamed the hills in every direction, while the merry clink of picks, the roar and rumble of dynamite explosions, and the chanting of the Basuto and Amatonga labourers in the mines proclaimed that the prophecies of Baines and Mauch were being fulfilled, and that at length the destiny of Africa was in a fair way of being fulfilled. It is little to be wondered at that I should have felt proud. For years, in common with many others, I had striven by my writings to convince the world of the mineral wealth of the country, and for years the efforts had fallen as it were to the ground; but now each day brings its triumph, and each hour its corroboration of the fact of Africa's stupendous wealth.

The bare plains, which five or six years ago were termed "Deserts," are now dotted with the tents of prospectors, from the doors of which, now and again, well-known pioneers and familiar comrades of travel shouted a cheery salutation. With a wave of the hand and a hearty "God-speed" we whirled on into the hazy distance, where new works constantly greeted us, and men with the stamp of health and hope on their faces laboured in certainty of success.

Now and again our wheels crashed over the deposits of conglomerate, locally called "banket." Presently the familiar name of Knox Bros. flashed on us from a huge sign-board, while the genial brothers met us with a hearty hand-grip and a welcome to the Transvaal. These pioneer colonists are to be met with in almost every part of South Africa; and where they are, there also is a post-office, a butchery, an hotel and a saw-mill. It is such men as these that build up the Empire, and uphold the prestige of Englishmen in the wild and lonely places.

On again for another hour through one continuous procession of waggons, carts, packmen, prospectors, and traders. Presently, the northern horizon appeared to rise and transform itself into a ridge, which proved to be the far-famed Witwatersrandt, while right on the sky-line the gables and streets of Johannesburg, ranged tier upon tier, could be seen gleaming under the rays of the sun.

A drive of thirteen miles brought us to the entrance of the city, and two miles further on, near its centre, we brought up in front of the post-office. The City of Gold in no way disappointed me. It was Saturday night, and well-behaved crowds of white, yellow and black men jostled each other in the streets and squares, while on every hand, single and double-storied houses bounded the view. Quite a throng of friends assembled to bid me welcome, while anxious porters principally of a half-and-half descent, snarled at each other over the luggage. Wending my way to an hotel, I found, to my dismay, that there was no room for me. After trying in several others, I at last obtained quarters, but not without the exercise of a certain amount of blarney. The house, it appeared, was full; editors, bank managers, stock brokers, engineers, assayers, adventurers, and travellers were all jumbled together in a happy unconsciousness of who was who. The bar, which occupied the end of the building, was conducted on principles of strict decorum. Owing to the extreme pressure on sleeping space I was not permitted to enjoy a room all to myself. The good-humoured, but somewhat intemperate, gentleman who slept in "the other corner," was somewhat addicted to coming home on all fours, at 3 a.m., and opening the door with his head. Barring this and a few stray fleas, and perhaps a score or so of bugs, I was very happy (I write now of the primitive days of Johannesburg).

After a wash and brush-up, I set forth to view the city; in the course of that walk, I met men from all parts of south, east, north, west, and central Africa: amongst whom I may specially mention Corry of Swazieland fame, and Stanley, who is a connection of the Congo traveller. A round of the bars, canteens, and music halls resulted in a most favourable impression of the town. Although the population of the place is estimated at about seven thousand, principally of the rough-and-ready sort, I only saw three fights and four drunk, all of which were of a very good natured description The Market Square, which is a large open space in the centre of the town, proved to be a most interesting study. Jewish pedlars auctioned "real" gold rings at two and sixpence a dozen, sets of silver studs at ninepence a dozen, and complete suits of clothes at fifteen shillings. Stalls bearing fruit, garden produce, and nick-nacks, were to be seen on every hand, and but for the total absence of napthaline lights, which were rendered unnecessary by reason of the fierce African sun, one might almost as well have been in Leather Lane. A blind and lame man was wheeled about on a barrow to the soul-stirring tunes of a hand-organ, whilst his daughter went round with the hat, in which I noticed silver coins only, copper being a coinage but little used in the Transvaal. In another corner of the Market Square, horses were being auctioned, the prices ranging from £4 10s. to £100. In yet another corner, stood ox-waggons heavily laden with firewood, which is still the main fuel, although coal of exceptionally good quality was at that time beginning to come forward as an article of commerce. Leaving the square, with its perspiring throngs, I turned into the office of the *Mining Argus*, one of the leading papers in the town. The editor, Mr. Deecker, of Du Val and Pretoria fame, was snugly quartered; while his office, which would have done no discredit to a provincial town of England, was well provided with the latest appliances of the age.

To speak of Johannesburg as having grown, conveys but a faint idea of the speed with which it has attained its present size. On the 20th September, 1886, the territory was proclaimed a public gold field, the township marked off and named. Capt. Von Brandis was appointed first Commissioner, and on the 8th of December, 1886, the first sale of building sites took place, and resulted in the realisation of £1,302; some of the stands in specially valuable positions brought £280. In January of 1887 another Government sale took place, resulting in the sum of £19,921. Gold laws and regulations where then framed and circulated, and licenses granted for prospecting and mining. Owing to the wonderfully rich finds, the settlement went on daily increasing until, on the occasion of my last visit 68 companys were established, with a nominal capital of £3,063,000 and 1,761 stamps at work, or in a fair way of commencing. It would be rash on my part to attempt any extensive geological explanation of the Witwatersrandt system at present; suffice it to say, that the gold-bearing strata of the region consists of reefs or lodes of conglomerate rock, formed of quartzose pebbles bedded solidly in disintegrated schists. This is cut out into claims for a distance of about fifty miles, and there is one almost continuous line of claims, numbering, at time of my last visit, 1,760; each claim measures 150 feet along the reef and 300 feet across it. The deposits in many cases are of great width,

Opening a Reef in Witwatersrandt Gold Fields.

and shafts of 300 feet and over have been sunk, proving the stability of the formation. Each claim may be considered as containing 90,000 cubit feet of gold-bearing stone, reckoning on 100 feet of depth only (and it has been proved to be over three times that), and reckoning 20 cubic feet to the ton, gives a total of 4,600 tons of banket in each claim. The average assays run considerably over 2 oz.; calculating on 1 oz. only, with a value of £3 10s. per ton, we have a gross claim value of £9,000; this, counting the number of claims, represents the grand figure of £15,840,000, and this, as I have already said, includes a surface valuation over a portion of the district only.

The amalgamation of gold in all countries and at all periods, has been, and always will be, a matter of considerable chemical difficulty. The Witwatersrandt formations, however, are singularly free from those re-agents so common in reefs of the ordinary description. Arsenic is almost unknown, sulphur occurs only in the faintest traces; antimony, so far as I could learn, being conspicuous by its absence. In fact, the chief difficulty appeared to be the recovery from the tailings of such gold as was chemically associated with the black sand.

I was especially privileged by the authorities of the Bank of Africa to enter their strong-room and feast my eyes on a fortnight's result of milling by fourteen small companies. Scattered on tables, floor, and benches lay piles of ingots of gold, while ranged in vessels along the walls stood heaps of spongy-looking retorted gold awaiting the smelter's attention. The value of this mass would be about £45,000.

CHAPTER XVI.

THE KOMATIE AND OTHER FIELDS.

THIS mining centre lies about thirty-five miles to the south of Barberton, and adjoins the frontier of Swazieland. It is connected with Delagoa Bay by a waggon road, the distance being about 120 miles. In the dry and healthy season this road is in considerable favour by carriers. Steynsdorp, the little township of the district, takes its name from Mr. Steyn, a Transvaal official. In July, 1885, mining life began in earnest, and it has gone on spasmodically ever since. There is no doubt whatever that the reefs in this vicinity have a great future before them. The population of the town is about 600; shops, hotels, churches, &c., are to be numbered amongst its institutions.

Of the other Gold Fields, I may mention those of Malmani, of Heidelberg, of Lydenburg, of the Blyde River, of the Tate, Matabeleland, Damaraland, Bechuanaland, Griqualand West and the Knysna. On each of these gold-bearing districts a book might well be written. The conditions are so similar to those which have already been dealt with, that such a course is unnecessary at the present time. Especial mention, however, might be made of the recent discoveries within the frontiers of our own colony of Natal. About forty miles east by north-east of the village of Greytown, in the uplands of Natal and on the northern frontier of the colony, there is a wild region, hemmed in by mountains, most of which range between 1,500 and 2,000 feet of altitude. The district presents to the traveller a constant series of magnificent combinations of mountain, forest, and river. The mimosa trees with their yellow buds, the wild pear trees with their wealth of snow-white blossom, the Kafir broom with its gigantic crimson flowers, clothe the mountains with a glory that must be seen to be appreciated; while the grass lands are literally emblazoned with daisies and lilies of every hue; here and there giant aloes spring from the earth and impart a wild and foreign aspect to the scene. Looking down into this valley, the tourist will appreciate the beauty and majesty of this portion of our Colonial Empire.

Taking horse from Greytown, where those animals may be hired at 14s. per day, six hours will suffice to bring us to this interesting place; two hours of a scramble down the rugged forest-clad hills will bring us to the verge of the Tugela River. If this scene was grand and interesting while spread out at one's feet, as it were, it assumes a tenfold interest when viewed from the river level.

The great mountains assume the most fantastic shapes, while the lonely forests with their intertwining creepers and branches form a barrier as it were between the traveller and the outer world; the river, lashed into foam, dashes along at an eight-mile speed over a bed strewn with boulders as large as average cottages. Wherever one looks quartz greets the eye: one has only to move the luxuriant foliage aside in order to reveal the delicately tinted masses of white, pink, blue or brown stone, some of which is gold bearing. The strata on the face of the hills on both sides of the river are not only very marked, but also very curious. The surface stone is principally trap rock, whinstone, and yellow clay-slate: that immediately below it varies—I saw yellow sandstone, conglomerate, and in places argillacious and mica-schists. Many of these strata are broken, and instead of lying flat as in their original state, they stand on end for miles, banking generally, but not always, white glassy quartz of the azoic period on their northern sides. Now and then these slabs are split and contain very interesting leaders which yield gold; deeper down, say, in some cases, six to eight feet from the surface, this quartz becomes spongy and assumes a burnt-clinker appearance. This latter always gave a good colour, both in my hands and in those of others who tried it. The lean or pitch of the reefs is to the southward, with an angle of about 45 deg., and their direction N.E. by S.W., generally speaking.

Turning down the river, the road (if the bouldery path might be so called) lies between huge conical and forest-clad mountains. Some of them were almost solid masses of quartz; others, again, gave promise of nothing beyond rocks and thorns. At intervals Kafir villages are to be seen, with their throngs of undraped, but exceedingly healthy and greedy inhabitants. No sooner does the traveller arrive at one of their settlements than he is surrounded by a gang of savages, who breathe hollow flatteries in his ears for the purpose of obtaining "bansello" (gifts). The word "U'shillin'" (shilling) is one that falls trippingly from their lips; babies lisp it, young fellows shout it, women squeal it, and old men thoughtfully and huskily whisper it. But my counsel to all and sundry is to be sternly economical, for the fame of a bestowed shilling will pass ahead, and life will be no longer a source of pleasure. If a native once gets the idea that the white man who sojourns within his gates is either lavish or "soft," there will be no longer any pleasure or profit in travel.

Several extensive workings for gold have been made in this beautiful and romantic region; while the Government, valuing the importance of the matter, have offered and awarded £1,000 for the discovery of payable gold. The valley of the Tugela will yet be a centre of mining importance, but apart from that, it is well worthy of a visit from the passing tourist.

On the other side of the river, in Zululand, considerable workings have been made and gold found, but as yet the results are not known.

CHAPTER XVII.

THE ZULUS AND ZULULAND.

NO play was ever so rich in dramatic incident, or so full of romantic adventure, as has been the history of this unfortunate and blood-stained country. For the past ten years, its frontiers have shifted from place to place with a bewildering rapidity, whilst the chief actors in the manufacture of its history have pursued such a perverse and erratic course as to render an intelligible and brief *resumé* of events a task of considerable difficulty. Having, as a lad, spent much time amongst the dusky warriors of the "land of Chaka," it is but natural that I should regard them with something more than philosophic interest, for I have dwelt in their villages, partaken of their food, and journeyed far and long in their company. Yet never, in all my experience of them, have I suffered even the slightest annoyance or inconvenience at their hands. In times of peril, they have stood bravely shoulder to shoulder with me, and in sickness they have tended me, faithfully and kindly.

The country, as will be shown further on, is now a portion of the British Empire. It is bounded on the south and southwest by the Colony of Natal; on the west and north-west by the New Republic (now the Transvaal); on the north by Amatongaland; and on the east by the Indian Ocean. Its population may be set down at 200,000. Its climate is, in the south and west, very healthy; but in the north and north-east, the East-coast Fever Belt commences. It possesses one harbour, St. Lucia Bay, as yet unopened.

The earliest records we have of the Zulus date from the close of the last century. At that time they were scattered over South-East Africa, between the Umzimvubu and Limpopo rivers, the Drakensberg and the sea. There appears to have been no union amongst them, each clan leading an independent life, ruled by its own hereditary chief. The land was fruitful, the climate mild and their herds numerous.

A Zulu Warrior.

Marriages were freely effected between the several tribes, and wars but little known. One of these tribes was ruled over by a supernatural sort of king called Zaweete. Another, and perhaps the leading clan, was under the control of a chief named Umtetwa. It appears, from national traditions, that this old warrior had two sons, named Tana and Godongwayo. The former, becoming impatient at his father's longevity, plotted his death; but, before his schemes could be carried into effect, the father found them out, and, dispatching a party of warriors, surrounded the kraal of the two young chiefs. Tana was killed, but Godongwayo managed, although wounded by a spear, which still quivered in his side, to leap the stockade wall and escape. When, next day, the story went abroad, Undulu, a sister of the youth, set out to search for her wounded brother; and, on finding him, nursed and watched over his safety until his wound was healed; then, supplying him with a kaross (robe), which possessed certain magical powers, sent him in safety out of the country. Many years passed over, yet the name of Godongwayo was not forgotten, and a belief sprung up that he would, some time or other, come back in great glory and triumph.

It is supposed that he made his way to Cape Town, where he learned something of European modes of warfare, for after an unmentioned number of years, he did in truth come back, mounted on a horse. By this time the old chief was dead and another ruled in his stead, but on the appearance of the prince, the usurper was removed, and Godongwayo, changing his name to Dingiswayo (the Wanderer), was proclaimed chief. Then commenced a reorganisation of the whole affairs of the tribe. An army, divided into companies, was established: badges of feathers and different coloured shields being used as distinguishing marks. Drill became the amusement of men and boys, and war and conquest their constant dream. Before very long, the system began to bear fruit: one tribe after another was crushed or amalgamated, and in a few years Dingiswayo was hailed as king of a considerable nation. By the judicious selection of his commanders, he contrived to go on piling up victories and adding to his power.

At this time a young Zulu, named Chaka, appeared before the king, for the purpose of obtaining admission to the army; this was accorded to him. Before very long he attracted attention by reason of his power of command, and when a vacant chieftainship offered, which happened to be over the

Zulu tribe, Chaka got the post. Following the lines of Dingiswayo, the new chieftain set about drilling his men and bracing them by all manner of exercises and hardships.

As years began to press heavily on Dingiswayo, Chaka's pretensions rose, and when that wise and temperate chief was gathered to his fathers, he seized the supreme command, and set out on a course of conquest. We have already made mention several times of the effect of this tyrant's terrible wars. Natal, at the time of the arrival of the first settlers, had been depopulated by him. The tribes of the district were scattered and starving, while in the west, Moselekatsie, one of his absconding generals, was carrying out his modest policy in slaughtering Bechuanas and emigrants whenever he got a chance.

But the tyrant's fate soon overtook the emperor, as he was by title, and in the year 1828 he fell a victim to the ambition of his kinsmen, one of whom, Dingaan by name, became ruler. This chief was, if anything, worse than the last, for he added treachery and cowardice to his other vices. It will be remembered that he caused the murder of Retief and the band of emigrant Boers who were his guests. In this act of treachery he signed his own death-warrant, for the Boers made an onslaught on him, and in flying from them he fell a victim to the spears of an independent nation called the Amaswazies, whose territories lay contiguous to, and north of Zululand.

The result of this disaster to the Zulus was, that the Boers claimed the region now known as Natal, and at the same time proclaimed an almost unknown native general, named Panda, king of the district lying between the Tugela River and the Limpopo. As war in the country was now almost an impossibility, the new king, it is said, sent marauding parties out to the north, where they came in collision with the Amaswazies, the Gazés, and other nations as far north as the Zambesi, and even to Lake Nyassa. Dr. Livingstone speaks of them several times, and always credits the depredations to the warriors with whom we are dealing. Among Panda's sons were two named Umbulazie and Cetywayo. The former was the recognised heir to the kingdom, but he was of an easy-going, unambitious nature, while Cetywayo (or to spell phonetically —Ketchwayo) was as fierce and blood-thirsty as Chaka.

Before long, matters between the two brothers became strained, and shortly afterwards, when old age began to tell on the king, civil war broke out. One party, the aggressive, being for Cetywayo, and the other for Umbulazie. The battle was fought over a space of forty miles, reaching from near the Royal Kraal to the Tugela River. Umbulazie's party were defeated, and it is supposed that he himself was carried away by the flooded boundary stream.

During the remainder of Panda's life, Cetywayo held the reins of government, and when the old king died, he was proclaimed Paramount Chief by his warriors, and crowned in state by the English Government.

Shortly afterwards, in 1879, Sir Bartle Frere, Her Majesty's High Commissioner in South Africa, conceived the idea that the Zulu power was a source of danger to the British Colony of Natal, and the result was the invasion and conquest of the land by British forces under Lord Chelmsford, Sir E. Wood, and other generals. The incidents of the war are too recent to need any especial mention here. The Zulu power was broken, Cetywayo captured and exiled for a time to the Cape Colony, and the country cut up into thirteen divisions, which were placed in charge of chiefs chosen by the Government. At the same time a strip of country along the frontier was reserved as a sort of No-man's-land, where those who feared to dwell under any of the petty chiefs might settle in peace and security. But alas for the so-called settlement, no sooner were the British officers' backs turned, than war and strife broke out between the districts, and in the space of a few years many thousand warriors fell in tribal conflicts. To crown all, Cetywayo was restored to his kingdom, with the exception of the strip of country along the frontier, which was called the Zulu Reserve, and another portion, which a chief named Usibepu ruled over.

Before many months had passed, war once more broke out, for it was quite impossible either to expect Cetywayo to rest content in his curtailed dominion, or Usibepu to settle down in peace while his late royal master's eyes were fixed with covetous desires on his territory. In order to secure the whip-hand of events, Usibepu made a grand attack on Cetywayo's main settlement, and in the resulting battle, the unhappy king was wounded and defeated. Attended by a small party of warriors, he took refuge in the depths of the Inkandhla Forest, which is situated near the Natal frontier, and in the midlands of his country.

Meanwhile Usibepu arrogated to himself a sort of royal power. Once more the British interfered, and after releasing Cetywayo, brought him down to the coast lands, where the camp was. But by some means or other, an enemy obtained access to him, and he died, it was supposed of poison. After this, Dinizulu, his son, was proclaimed king. Usibepu continued his aggressions to such an extent, that the boy-king, despairing of help from England, appealed to the Boers to aid him in destroying his adversary. Those astute and land-hungry settlers were not slow to respond. Entering into a contract to beat Usibepu, in consideration of certain land concessions, they, to the number of 600 or 1,000, swept down from the Transvaal, and after a severe engagement, shattered the forces of the turbulent Zulu prince. History repeated herself here, for Dinizulu soon learned that in crushing one foe by employing an alien race, he had raised another who would practically have the same effect on him, *i.e.*, swallow up his kingdom. After sundry squabbles, the Boers settled on the inland parts of the country, and formed the new Republic, which has since been incorporated with the Transvaal.

By this means, Zululand was so reduced in area as to be practically ruined. So in order to save the remnant of the nation, Her Majesty's Government, in 1887, formally annexed the country, and took the Zulus permanently under protection as a portion of the Empire.

CHAPTER XVIII.

Customs and Legends of Zululand.

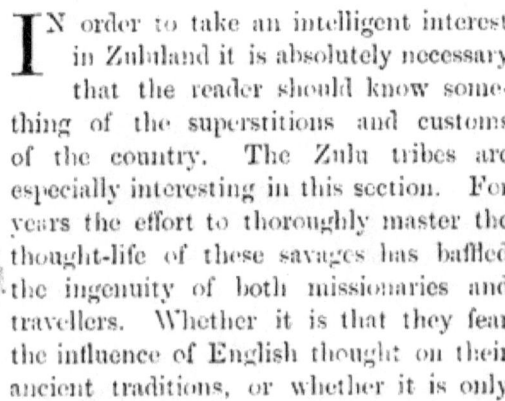
Zulu Prophetess.

IN order to take an intelligent interest in Zululand it is absolutely necessary that the reader should know something of the superstitions and customs of the country. The Zulu tribes are especially interesting in this section. For years the effort to thoroughly master the thought-life of these savages has baffled the ingenuity of both missionaries and travellers. Whether it is that they fear the influence of English thought on their ancient traditions, or whether it is only a natural reserve, I know not; but the fact is, that a Zulu will go to any amount of trouble to conceal the beliefs of his fathers. However, by a long residence in the country, and by much conversation with the late Dr. Oftebro and others, I have been enabled to collect much interesting information, a summary only of which can be given here. According to the most cherished traditions of Zululand, which may be only told with bated breath, the creation of the nations took place in this wise :—

Long ago, when the hills were young, the Great Spirit. Inkuluinkulu, looked on the earth, which was without men; presently, as he looked, there came a rustling in the reeds, and the tribes of the earth bursting forth, climbed out on the dry land and spread themselves over the country. The Great Spirit having regarded them carefully, approved of them; and, in order to mark his approval and express it to them, called up, as a messenger, the Inwabo (chameleon), and dispatched it, saying, "Go and tell the nations that death shall never come amongst them; that they shall live for ever." Setting forth on his journey, the chameleon, who is a slow traveller, put off time on the road by eating berries. During this interval the Great Spirit changed his mind, on account of the wickedness of the people, and calling up the Intulu (lizard), he dispatched it, saying, "Go tell the people, if the other message has not been delivered, that death shall be their portion." With lightning speed the lizard went on his mission, and, passing the chameleon, who was still loitering delivered his dread message. The people, not knowing anything of the pain of death, replied, "It is well; we accept the command." Presently, after the pains of death had terrified them, the chameleon arrived, and, delivering his useless message, was declared by the people to be a curse from that day forth; hence his tottering gait and constantly changing colour.

Witchcraft is another of their institutions, which is much used—or rather misused—by the rulers for purposes of personal aggrandisement. This subject divides itself into several sections, the worst of which is called the U'Swellaboi. This especial kind of witch or wizard is possessed of the spirit of murder, and treats his victims in somewhat the same fashion as the celebrated "Jack the Ripper," who attracted so much attention in Whitechapel, in 1888. Another description of witch or wizard is alleged to have the power of causing the death of whomsoever he will, by the exercise of charms and curses; others, again, have the power of keeping off rain. In order to cope with these, a race has sprung up, called Inyanga-u-ku-Bula, or prophets and seers. These are the national ministers of vengeance on all evil ones. When anything goes wrong, such as a continued drought, an epidemic amongst the cattle or people, a national disaster or defeat, they are ordered to Bula or prophesy, and detect the wicked one who is maliciously causing the trouble, for it is a canon of the Zulu faith, that no calamity, not even death, can occur without the aid of some Umtagatie or witch. Now and again, when a private man's herds of cattle attract the king's attention, it may happen that he will be accused by the wizards and slaughtered, his flocks and herds being, of course, confiscated.

The king, by virtue of his royal office, is supposed to have supreme control not only over all mankind but over the elements. It is by his command that the seasons come and go, and he has power to influence the rain and sunshine. When, by any chance, a long drought overtakes the land, the nation invariably appeal to the king for help, and the ingenuity exercised by him on such occasions is extremely amusing. I have more than once noticed a potentate's eye critically studying the heavens while such appeals were being

Zulu Village or Kraal.

made to him. By temporising, he generally contrives to give Nature time to come to his aid, and then, when the rains are lashing down, he looks upon the people about him with the air of a man who has done the right thing. In the event of the rain still holding off, however, somebody is condemned to death, and folk are contented.

Their marriage laws are extremely interesting; they are, of course, polygamists, the first wife, in ordinary cases, having authority over the others. Their dwellings are beehive-like structures of grass, and each woman enjoys one to herself and family. The first wife's hut or house is always placed on the right-hand side of that of her husband, the second on the left, and so on, until the village assumes a horseshoe shape;

the centre of this is occupied by an enclosure, called the "sebia" or cattle kraal. Outside the houses there is a stockade, which serves as a protection against attacks by man or beast. This little digression is necessary, in order to pave the way for the description of the marriage ceremony. When a youth realises that his heart is no longer his own, he announces the fact to his father or his uncle; the matter is talked over and discussed in all its lights, and, should there be no objection to the maiden's family, a messenger, driving an ox as an offering, is despatched to her father's village. Should the overture be received with respect, negotiations are entered upon touching the number of cattle to be paid by the young man to his adored one's father, as a sort of indemnity for the trouble and expense of having reared her. This question settled, preparation becomes the order of the day; both sides have new songs and dances. The bride elect collects her stock of mats, spoons, calabashes, earthen pots, &c., which she has been preparing. When the eventful day arrives, the bride, attended by a large following decked out in their very best plumes and beads, set out for the bridegroom's kraal, which they only enter at night. Certain huts are set apart for them, and no one of the bridegroom's family must look upon their approach. All night long the maiden wanders about the village wailing, or pretending to do so. Next morning, the husband, his family and friends, take up their position in the interior enclosure, or cattle kraal; the bride and her party follow them and take up a position opposite. At this point a spear is put into her hand, and, while she holds it, some water is poured into a gourd, which she throws at her husband; at the same time she advances and strikes the women of his household, thereby symbolising that, for the future, she has authority over them; she then breaks the shaft of the spear as a token of her submission to her master. She then suddenly makes a rush as though to escape, but the young men of her husband's party seize her and bring her back a captive; after this the girls of her family wail for the one who is no more of them; and then

ZULU BOYS.

(From a Photograph by the Author.)

come feasting, dancing, and sometimes fighting. No widow who remarries is permitted to break the spear. The mother-in-law joke of civilisation is carefully guarded against among these barbarians; for if a man had ten wives, and if the father of each wife had also ten wives, the result would be one hundred (100) mothers-in-law. Such a condition of affairs requires special legislation, and we find here that no mother may enter her married daughter's hut or partake of her food under the most awful penalties; she may not even look upon the face of her son-in-law; and, in the event of occasion requiring her advice, such as illness or child-birth, she may, on the request of her son-in-law, conveyed by messenger, converse with him over a fence each turning their back towards the other. According to Kafir law, if no children result from the union the wife may be returned or compensation claimed.

When a child is born, it is fed for the first few days upon sour milk, and it is only, I think, on the third day at earliest that it obtains its natural sustenance. In the rearing of children the natives show great wisdom—the little dots are neither coddled nor neglected. When they get a little older, say eight or nine years of age, the boys are expected to herd the calves and the girls to help their mothers about the house. It is an interesting fact that the lying-in period of Zulu women seldom exceeds three days; in fact, I have seen many scores labouring in the cornfields the day after their confinement. This, perhaps, is owing to the fact that Nature is allowed to work her own cure. The men devote themselves almost entirely to warlike exercises and the hunt, the only domestic department proper to them being the milking of the cows, a duty which no woman under any circumstances will undertake. It is especially important that the traveller and settler should be reserved, yet kindly, in his behaviour both to those who serve him and those amongst whom he travels. As I said some time ago, I have always received the utmost consideration and kindness, not only at the hands of the Zulus, but from all the tribes with whom I have been brought into contact. I attribute this mainly to the fortunate fact of my acquaintanceship with their language and customs. All African natives, and especially the Zulus, are quite willing to admit the superior wisdom and ingenuity of the white man. One must abstain from exhibitions of temper, excesses of any kind, or an appearance of indolence. Like all untutored men, they will, when they can, take advantage, but this is easily guarded against. The average wage of a Zulu ranges from 10s. to £1 per month, food inclusive, which will cost about

A Zulu Chief.

the same; for this consideration, he will serve you faithfully night and day. His idea of complete attire is strictly confined to the Limited Liability Act; a girdle of cat skins around his waist, a blanket to sleep in at night, and a feather to stick in his wool are quite sufficient. The girls, until of a marriageable age, go quite naked, and, as a consequence, are healthy, athletic, and happy. Their principal diet consists of maize, millet, sour milk, and flesh. Fish they regard with abhorrence and will only handle it under protest; fowls, also, used to be regarded as undesirable, but this prejudice is disappearing.

CHAPTER XIX.

SWAZIELAND AND THE SWAZIES.

AS Swazieland is rapidly coming into prominent notice, both as a gold field and a hunting ground, it deserves especial attention. The geographical importance of the country can scarcely be over-rated, lying as it does between the Transvaal and the sea, while in a geological and mineralogical sense, it is a veritable treasure land. The boundaries of the countries may be laid down as follows:—North, west and south by the Transvaal, and east by the Lu Bomba Mountains, which separate it from Portuguese Africa. An important trade route runs right through the country from Delagoa Bay to the New Scotland district of the Transvaal, and it is the illegal traffic here which is principally to blame for the leakage in the Natal and Cape Colony customs revenues in the winter or dry seasons.

The country measures, roughly speaking, about 150 miles by 80, and is of an oval shape, its greatest length being north and south. Its physical geography partakes of the nature of the rest of South Africa, *i.e.*, steppes or terraces, two of which are within the boundaries of the country. The highest level, which lies somewhat lower than that of the Transvaal, is open and grassy, with occasional forests and numerous rivers, chief amongst which may be mentioned the Assagia, Great and Little Usutus, Inkompeece, Umbeloose (Black and White) and

Komatie. There are countless smaller streams flowing into these.

The lower stretches of the country are covered almost throughout with dense and tangled forests of thorn trees, amongst which innumerable herds of game of all kinds move in battalions—lions, leopards, wolves (hyenas), jackals, wild dogs and ant-bears, koodoo, veldebeeste, buffalo, giraffe, eland, red-deer, reed-boks, and a long catalogue of others are to be had at very little trouble. Fever at certain times of the year (summer) renders this rather a dangerous locality. The rivers, before they gain these plains, unite for the most

Darker Buck.

part, and flow through it at considerable interval; as a consequence, water is often not to be had for a stretch of fifty miles or more. Travellers would do well to fit themselves with vessels of sufficient capacity to stave off thirst until these dry reaches have been passed. The productions of the country are similar to those of Zululand.

The Swazie nation is doubtless a branch of the great organisation commenced by Dingiswayo. Their traditions record that they were established where they now are, and in the region to the north now occupied by the Boers, about the time of Chaka's glory. They almost exterminated the Makatele tribe, and conquered the Amatongas, who pay a sort of tribute to them up to the present time.

The first king whose history is authenticated is Umswazie, the father of the present king. Lu Donga took his place when he died; but Lu Donga was found dead in his kraal one day, and rumour credited his mother with the crime, her idea, it is asserted, being to wed the prime minister, and bear an heir; while all this was taking place, she hoped to reign as regent, but the loyalists at once elected Umbandine, Lu Donga's brother, the present king, and made war on the plotting and unnatural mother, who fell in battle. With her there died over three thousand warriors in one day, I have been told. From that time (1870) to the present (1888), Umbandine has reigned in almost unbroken peace.

Touching the people, they are a strange jumble of good and bad. Greedy to the last degree towards strangers, they are lavish to their friends, whether they be black or white. Brave when actually put to it, they have shown in recent years a nervous fear of war, and would rather lose ground than fight the fillibustering crew of Dutch adventurers who, from time to time, sweep down on them and nibble away the edges of their realm.

The Government is a limited monarchy, consisting of a king, prime minister, and council of chiefs. The land is national property, and the disposal of it lies with the king and council. As the manners and customs of the people are closely related to those already detailed in the Zulu section, no special mention need be made of them. But in order to impart an idea of what one must expect while travelling in their country, I will relate some of the events of my recent journey of exploration. After purchasing waggons, oxen and necessary fittings—such as camp stores, picks, shovels, pots, pans and kettles, and engaging as driver, a solemn-faced Zulu, who was learned in the art of swinging a thirty-foot whip and guiding a team of cattle over the roadless wilds—we started, accompanied also by two or three other attendants; after a couple of weeks' journeying through Natal and Zululand, I found myself outspanned on the southern bank of the Pongola River, which was "up." To attempt the passage would have been fatal; for in addition to being flooded, it was well stocked with quick-sands, while an occasional alligator lifted his expectant nose out of the stream. While sitting engaged in considering my position, I heard behind me a musical whistling of whips, co-mingled with the alto voices of sundry Kafir boys. Presently a heavy lumbering Dutch waggon, to which a span (team) of oxen was attached, came rolling over the stony hill side and halted beside me. Seated on the front box was a venerable Boer of magnificent dimensions. He had a long, flowing white beard, a sun-burnt face, and wore cord clothes, untanned shoes, and smelt most unmistakably of gin.

Approaching me and extending a hand as big almost as a leg of mutton, he in a husky voice asked God to bless me; he then invited himself to dine with me. Over this meal my new friend, whom we will call for convenience and brevity sake Myneer Otto Von Blisterschlapen, proposed a union of expeditions. Seeing that he owned a fine team of cattle that might be available in helping me over a bad bit of country or a deep river I consented. So pledging each other in another cup of tea, we retired to our respective couches in great good humour. Next day, as the river still continued impassable, we resolved to cruise further upstream in search of a better crossing. The journey proved like so many others that South African travellers have to endure—full of hard work, under a burning sun, and over miserable roads, but the indescribable charm of the country and the free open life, more than counterbalanced our vexations. By sunset we had found a safer place to cross, and after a few hours' rest plunged into the stream, which is broad, deep and rapid. An hour's struggle saw us standing exhausted and dripping on the northern side. The ascent from the river was like the path of life, narrow and thorny, with pitfalls on every hand.

Having gained the summit, we had a magnificent view into the valley of the White River, so called because of the immense deposits of marble in the vicinity. A journey of ten miles brought us to the edge of this river, over which I passed in safety, whilst Myneer Blisterschlapen stuck fast in the mud.

His wheels became buried to the axles and sank deeper each moment; his oxen got sullen and would not pull; his driver broke his fifteen foot bamboo whip-stick, whilst the little Hottentot boy, who led the oxen, lifted up his piping voice and wept, for he knew that lashes were laid up for him, as the whole disaster was of his bringing about. Despite our efforts the huge structure of canvass and planks slowly and majestically capsized, drawing from the Dutchman as it did so a deep and hollow remark, which I may not translate. After nearly a day's labour, we righted the waggon and passed on to a little spruit, where a small colony of pioneer Dutch were settled.

This region comprises a narrow strip of territory which was ceded by the King of Swazieland to the English when the Transvaal Republic was a British Colony, for the purpose of putting a belt of English farmers between his nation and the Zulus. On the restoration of the Transvaal to the Dutch, this district, of course, came into the hands of the Boers.

That night, as I was retiring to my customary perch, I was disturbed by one of the settlers, who implored me to come and see his wife, who was ill. Resuming my garments, I followed my guide to a small stone hut, in which I found about fourteen unkempt children, three dirty young ladies in tears, and two grizzled specimens of the genus Fillibuster. On a pallet in the corner laid the sufferer. She was a monstrous mountain of flesh, and was sobbing with the face-ache. Mixing a little liquid ammonia and sweet oil, equal parts, which forms hartshorn, and telling her husband to rub it in, I hurriedly took my departure, for the smell of the place was sickening.

Passing on from here, still in a northerly direction, we towards evening sighted another Boer camp, where we halted. As my fellow-traveller claimed kinship with this lot, we went in to pay our respects to the ladies and gentlemen of the household. The former I found seated in a circle on the ground in the backyard engaged in cobbing mealies (removing the grains of Indian corn from the cobs). The lord of creation leant against the back door of the house and smoked. He

M

was a tall, grey man, with a thoughtful, though a dirty, face. His long, flowing locks fell in tangled masses on his shoulders, and a pair of sharp grey eyes flashed from under a set of heavy and fierce eyebrows. Hostility was plainly stamped on his face, for I was an Englishman and he a Fillibuster. Before very long, he commenced to boast of his prowess in the Boer War of 1881. According to his own account, it was from his unerring rifle that all the most fatal bullets sped at Amajuba and Lang's Neck. His cheer it was that encouraged the Boers and crushed the English. In the course of his conversation he told me that he hated an Englishman like poison; and if he could starve, shoot, poison, or injure one of them he would consider himself doing the God of Boerdom a service. After assuring him that I admired him for his outspokenness, we parted—I to my camp, he to his thoughts and his everlasting pipe.

This specimen of humanity and his class are quite distinct from the Boers who are settled in the Colonies and the more trodden parts of the two Republics.

The next day we won our way to the bank of the Assagai River, which may now be called the southern frontier of Swazieland. Crossing this stream, which has a bouldery bed, we pushed on, over the highlands of Swazieland, without trouble until we gained the bank of the Inkompeece River (the place of leopards and wolves). As this stream is about fifty yards across, with a bed of boulders, over which about five feet deep of snow-white foaming water sweeps, I resolved to halt until morning, and cross with freshly-rested cattle, for to "stick fast" in such a place would mean disaster and death. Next morning I swam across, in order to test the speed and depth, and finding it so much more dangerous than I had supposed, I resolved to pass on on foot to a Mission Station which I had heard of, in hopes of obtaining another span of oxen, for my Dutch friend had resolved to settle amongst his kinsfolk, whom I had just left.

Meeting a passing Swazie on the hill, I learned that a

trader, the only one in the country, was encamped within six miles of me. Turning in the direction indicated, I soon sighted his camp, which was situated on the other side of the Umhlatan River. Crossing, I learned to my delight that the white trader was my old comrade in arms, Harry Darke Bayly. Then, behold, there was joy in the land as we sat down on a log and shook hands with each other. Harry's cattle were sent back for my waggon, which arrived that night in safety. Next day a notable hunter, named Martine, having heard from the natives of my arrival, came up to see me, and together we journeyed on. That night we encamped on the crest of the far-famed M'Kaiyan Mountains.

CHAPTER XX.

SWAZIELAND AND THE SWAZIES.

AT this point the country falls suddenly from the High Veldt, with its bare grassy and stony hills to a depth of about two thousand feet, where the Usutu River can be seen meandering like—

"A silver cord
Through all, and curling loosely both before
And after, over the whole stretch of land."

It was a fairy scene, wrapped as it was in its hazy mantle of soft and luminous grey, with the mysterious hills beyond it, and in the nearer valley, close apparently at our feet, the great timbered mountain crests, with their frowning fronts of gold quartz and their soft-toned forest slopes. There, right in sight, lay the "great place" of the king, and the villages of the nation. Later in the evening the mist lifted from the eastward, and disclosed the Lu Bomba Mountains, hazy and unsubstantial looking; here it is that the lion has his lair and the slave-dealer his sanctuary. The moon rose very late that night, yet, as she looked down into the huge chasm and tinged the cliffs with her soft silvery light, I could not but resolve to do all that one man can do to avert the ruin that threatens the land, and even now advances greedily towards it, as we have seen in the outposts of the Boer fillibusters whom I had just left.

The descent of the M'Kaiyan range is an event in one's life. For years I had heard the fame of it, and travelling natives had told me that it was "a place for birds and not for men." The round and jolly face of Martine lengthened somewhat as he looked down the hill and then regarded the wheels of my desert ship. Selecting a promising-looking dry gully we plunged over the edge. Fastening ropes to the hand rails, Martine and I hung on and strove to check the headlong descent, while Bayly stood to the break like a hero. Away we went, for going down M'Kaiyan is like going into action—the less one reflects on probable dangers the better. Reach after reach was passed in safety; at times my rope-fellow and I had to take flying leaps, in order to keep pace with the rapid descent of the waggon. When about halfway down, we struck a huge boulder with such a shock as to send us rolling heels-over-head; recovering ourselves, on we went again. Several times the cattle fell headlong, and cut themselves on the sharp-edged stones. The yells of the drivers and the shouts of encouragement directed to the Kafirs and the cattle, were taken up by the echoes before and behind us. But we had but scant time to listen to echoes; a deep watercourse crosses the track just where it is most sidling, steep and stony. Into it we went with a crash, out of it with a cheer, and on again with a dash —down, down, down! We were in the forest belt by this time; wild cactus trees lifted up their arms as though in surprise at the unwonted disturbance, the rock rabbits crouched in their nests, and the convolvuli-draped waterboom trees rustled their over-laden branches in welcome to us, for once more we stood in the region of palms and ferns, of flowers and sunshine.

The next day brought us to the bank of the Great Usutu River, which at this point separates into two arms, enclosing an island of about two miles by half-a-mile. Crossing the southern arm, we pitched camp for a few days, in order to explore the beauties of the district. On the southern bank of the river I noticed several reefs, which, however, I had not time to test. On the island itself, and on the mainland to the north, copper ore appeared; while in the last I found several traces of silver. The appearance of the country was most picturesque and impressive, the mountains being all of great height, and crowned with beetling cliffs; while the valleys, for the most part, are clothed with one continuous forest, in the glades of which, countless flowers of every hue are to be met with.

Passing on again refreshed from our rest, we, after ten hours' steady travelling, arrived at "Lu Dittin," the village of Sandhlana, the Prime Minister. Before long that dignitary himself appeared, attended by about forty warriors. Seating himself in my tent, he bade me welcome to the "*Land of Gangwan.*" Sandhlana is a light made, thin man, with a thoughtful face and a deliberate manner of speech. The first salutation over, he asked, " When is England coming to help her children? we are being eaten by the wolves from the west (pointing towards the Transvaal), and yet, as they are white, we dare not make war on them, knowing full well that the English chiefs in Natal and Cape Town would take part with their own colour against ours." On my replying that the Queen knew nothing of this trouble, he seemed surprised, and asked " What are her chiefs and governors doing?" After a long and interesting chat he withdrew, and sent me presents of meat and corn. An hour or two afterwards, the king's brother, Umkopolo, a captain in the " Hlavella," or Royal Regiment of Spearmen, approached, and delivered a long and friendly message from the king—who is a very different man to the anointed of Pondoland, who visited me while travelling near St. John's. Here there is real power, authority and state, simple perhaps, but none the less real. Closely following the prince's visit came more corn and meat, together with a few fowls and some milk.

Next day, having sent carriers ahead, I rode over to see the king. The " Great Place " (Umbegelin) is close to the village of Sandhlana, and overlooking the tiny brook Untillan. Towering over it is the Umtemba Mountain, with its refuge caves and maze of bouldery roads, where in times of peril the royal family retire for security. The settlement itself consists of about 600 huts, of the usual beehive character. The portion set aside for the king and his wives and servants, is situated near the upper side of the central enclosure, or cattle-pen; while flanking it on all sides are long semi-circular rows of stockaded dwellings, devoted to the accommodation of the regimental detachments in attendance on the king. On arriving at the main entrance I dismounted, and my horse was led away by an attendant. Followed by my four natives, I was taken into the cattle-pen, where, surrounded by a throng of

Royal Kraal or Great Place, Swaziland.

over a hundred men, stood the king. In appearance he is tall and portly; his skin, like all the royal stock of South-East Africa, is of a light copper colour, his eyes are large and expressive, and his hands and feet are, considering his size, remarkably small.

Turning, he came forward to meet me, and after shaking hands, repeated the Prime Minister's welcome. " We want Englishmen, and Englishmen only, here," he said; " but instead, we get these," indicating a couple of Boers, who were standing about a hundred and fifty yards off, awaiting his pleasure to grant them an interview. After a little time he signified that they might approach, which they did. Their mission was to crave a few blades of grass, *i.e.*, the right to graze their cattle and squat on his uplands. In return for the permission, which was granted, they presented him with a horse, a gun, and four blankets. The king knew well that he was virtually selling his birthright for a mess of potage, but, as he explained, there was no other way of preserving peace; and be it remembered that this man had and has absolute command over at least 15,000 gallant warriors, who have more than once, in England's service, during the Seccacunie War, proved their bravery and devotion.

Turning into his private dwelling, we partook of some steamed meat, beer and sour milk. After a couple of hours' gossip on the affairs of the world generally, I withdrew and returned to camp, having made an appointment for an official interview next day. (I was at that time acting as correspondent for the press). Next morning I found the king and his counsellors assembled in state when I arrived, and took the seat assigned to me beside him. Sandhlana, the prime minister, then rose, and in a low, but very clear voice, pointed out the danger the country was in from invasion by irregular gangs of fillibusters. "What do you propose as a remedy?" I enquired. "You are a writer of letters in the papers," was the reply. "We wish you to make our condition known to the English people, both in Natal, the Cape, and in England. When the Government know of our trouble, they will aid us; for General Wood, when here, on his way to Delagoa Bay, promised that if ever we were in danger, the Queen would act as our friend and serve us, as we did her generals, when they called upon us." In answer, I said that I would do my best to make the matter public; at the same time, I suggested that a petition to the High Commissioner would perhaps, if it came straight from the king, serve a good purpose. This petition was then drafted, and signed by Umbandine and several of his chiefs. I forwarded it to Colonel Cardew, the Sub-Commissioner in the Zulu Reserve, and there, as far as I was concerned, the matter ended. After several months spent in this vicinity, I started for the hunting grounds, where those interested in sport may perhaps care to accompany me.

CHAPTER XXI.

THE HUNTING GROUNDS OF SWAZIELAND.

EASTWARD HO! Away down from the open hills, lichened rocks, and flower-strewed prairies, to the wilderness of forest, where the game dwelleth and where the nights are made hideous by reason of the howls of the beasts of prey. After passing the "Monain Kraal," where one of the late king's widows resides, we entered a valley where no stones, save crystalline quartz, are to be seen. Towards evening of the same day, we passed a number of deserted villages whose inhabitants had been killed off on a charge of witchcraft. Calling a halt for a few hours we pressed on again, in order to, if possible, reach water; this, however, we failed in doing, and it was noon of next day before either cattle or men could slake their thirst.

The next night saw us encamped in a beautiful park-like country, where we found abundant signs of koodoo, zebra, and lions. After this we had to remove the hood of the waggon, in order to get through the forest, for the tracks were what our American cousins would call eye-openers.

The stone in this region is quite different to that over which we had previously journeyed. Great lodes of ironstone crossed path at frequent intervals, and my unfortunate waggon stood a good chance of being rattled to pieces. The country soon began to form into long east and west ridges, between each of which were slimy-looking pools covered with green spawn; to get over these was no small labour, and it was with delight that we struck the thick forest and level plains again.

Going ahead in order to pick out an open course, I found

myself suddenly confronted with a large herd of zebra, koodoo, and veldebeeste; they were scarcely a hundred yards distant, and stood gazing with curiosity at the approaching waggon; before I could get my gun ready, however, they went off to deeper shades. In another hour we pitched camp in an open space, and felling some thorn trees formed a circle of the branches round the camp, in order to protect the cattle against any possible attack. The sky was cloudless, the air balmy, and but for the almost continuous howling of the wolves, we should have slept comfortably and soundly.

Next morning, leaving the waggon in charge of some friendly Swazies, I set off on foot for a celebrated cave on the Umbelusie River, about fifteen miles from camp. Accompanied by Bayly, Martine and four native hunters, we had a merry time of it, and before eleven o'clock had killed more meat than we cared to carry. Early in the afternoon we arrived at the cave, which we found well stocked with animal life; for I killed a sixteen-feet-long boa-constrictor, while Bayly discovered two young wolves, and hosts of vampire bats. Having cleared and swept up the cave, which is simply a pile of conveniently arranged sandstone rock, we sat down to supper, and then lay down to sleep. About midnight we were suddenly aroused by the loud and angry snarling of a lion, who, doubtless attracted by the smell of the fresh meat, had climbed on top of the cave, with dishonest intentions; finding himself baffled, he gave vent to his displeasure. The three of us turned out, and delivered some well-meant but ill-directed bullets in his direction; it being dark as pitch, we failed to catch sight of him. He withdrew to a safer distance, however, and spent the rest of the night—to judge by the tone of his voice—in high displeasure.

By the very earliest streak of dawn we were *en route*, each taking a native hunter and a separate road. My native led me in a bee-line eastward, where, before long, we were hammering away in good earnest at the red deer. But I was never much of a Nimrod, so, ordering the native to hold his hand, I passed on still further, being intent on obtaining a sketch of the mountain ranges.

While pushing my way through the tall grass, I heard a sudden rustling right in front. On pausing, the rustling ceased; so creeping forward stealthily, followed by the hunter, I raised myself to peep at what sort of creature we were disturbing. At the same moment a black-faced lion did likewise. We were not ten yards apart, and by all appearance he was as much disconcerted as we were, for, bristling his mane in a threatening manner, he gave a low sniff and stalked off, for which I was duly thankful. When he had attained a sufficient distance to insure me an opportunity of placing three or four bullets at least, I opened fire, but his majesty would not wait. As I was in no especial need of his company, we were both satisfied to allow the intimacy to drop, which it did. Returning to the cave, we found the others snugly reclining on rugs, imbibing steaming coffee, and regarding with extreme complacency a ghastly row of slaughtered deer.

Having dried the flesh, we returned to the waggon and started off on a short visit to the Lu Bomba Mountains, where, I was informed, a company of white and coloured slave-dealers were carrying on their traffic. Owing to a slight miscalculation of distance, we once again suffered some inconvenience from want of water; but after twenty-four hours of thirst, gained the foot of the mountain and found a pool. Halting close to it, we sent a man down for some. When the precious liquid came to hand, we were not surprised to find it thick, slimy and tepid. Still, for even that we were "truly thankful," and not only drank with relish, but baked bread and boiled meat in it.

Next morning, just as we were on the point of starting, dense clouds of smoke came whirling down the slopes towards us, and a few moments later the whole mountain range seemed to become a mass of flames. The natives were hunting, and, in order to drive the game, they had fired the prairie. The conflagration seemed to leap over the tall dry grass, great tongues of flame floated in the air, while countless birds fell quivering into the fiery mass, and game of the smaller sort went skimming on at top speed; but not for long, for as suddenly as the flames appeared on one hand, a band of native hunters sprang out on the other. Clad in their fluttering girdles of fur, with their lithe and sinewy forms, they seemed very demons, as they dashed hither and thither, spearing or firing at the deer. In half-an-hour the fire was past and the hunters out of sight. We found the slaves in their huts and stockades, near the Umbelusie Poort, or pass of the mountain, and I satisfied myself that the traders were in truth dealing in boys and girls, whom they either purchased or stole, on one side of the mountain, to sell on the other.

Dead Buffalo.

One might purchase a boy, of ten or twelve years of age, from £8; while girls were worth from £10 to £15, according to their age and appearance. I reported the matter at the time, in the Colonial press, with considerable effect; for, after the to them most undesirable publicity, they found it convenient to scatter and dodge about the country for a time.

While in this region I obtained some good partridge shooting, but an injury to my right hand and arm prevented a full enjoyment of the sport. Besides, my duties and anxieties kept me hard at work, oftentimes all day and far into the night.

The Boer fillibusters, having heard of the king's public appeal through me, were also very active; but, as they failed in their attempts to silence me, I bear them no ill will.

Before closing with Swazieland, I may mention that the gold discoveries within recent years have been most extensive and rich. The Forbes concession, 50,000 acres in extent, is at present being worked, while several other mills are in course of erection.

DELAGOA BAY.

(From a Photograph by the Author.)

CHAPTER XXII.

A Peep at East Africa—Delagoa Bay—Lorenzo Marques—Railways—Amatongaland.

THE Port and Colony of Delagoa is situated about three hundred miles north of Port Natal, and eleven hundred miles from Cape Town. It forms the southernmost of the Portuguese possessions in East Africa. The coast between it and Durban possesses but few features of picturesque interest, the shore being flat in many places. From Cape Vidal to Inyack Island the sea line trends in a north-easterly direction, and possesses an almost continuous series of sand hills, ranging from fifty to one hundred feet in height. After passing Inyack Island, which will receive attention in due course, the first object that attracts the traveller's attention is a long flat-topped ridge named Reuben Point. It has an elevation of two hundred feet. The sides, which are precipitous, consist of a superstratum of red earth, beneath which the yellow clay shines out in strong contrast; here and there, water ruts have been formed, and the bright red earth having been washed down them, presents a curious pillar-like appearance at a distance. The vegetation on the table land is very beautiful, consisting of bright green sward, plentifully besprinkled with clusters of mimosa and other trees, amongst which is situated the trim quarters of the South African Telegraph Company's officials.

After a mile or two of voyaging over smooth water, we arrived at the town, which is situated on a low bank. This is the far-famed and much-abused Lorenzo Marques. The first object that arrested my attention, was the red tiled fort over which floated the royal standard of Portugal. A long column of white smoke flew out from an embrasure in its walls, and the heavy boom of a gun roared a hoarse welcome to the good ship *Danube*, of the Union Company's service, which bore in addition to the Mails the genial Captain Edward Baynton, R.N.R., General Brownrigg, C.B., together with myself and attendants. It was the purpose of the first mentioned to extend the operations of the Union Steam Ship Company in that direction. General Brownrigg was on a simple holiday excursion, whilst my duties were to describe and illustrate the place.

As the present development of the mineral wealth of South Africa has added considerably to the interest attaching to this place, and as it is, in a sense, one of the routes to the Gold Fields, it deserves considerable attention at our hands.

The discovery of the bay was due, as in the case of Natal, to the explorations of Vasco de Gama, in 1497. It extends from Cape Inyack to about latitude 25 deg. 35 min. south, a distance of twenty-five miles. The principal part of this distance is obstructed by shoals, caused by the deposits ejected from the rivers which flow into the bay. Inside of Cape Inyack and to the northward of it, Inyack Island is situated. It is six miles long by three and a-half broad. The north-western part of the island is low and encloses a shallow lagoon, which is fronted by Elephant Island on the west and open to the southward. Port Melville is formed by the shelter afforded by these two islands.

Shefeen Island, on the other side of the bay, is long and low, trending E.N.E. and W.S.W. It is covered with dense bush, and is said at one time to have abounded in game. There are dangerous shallows and reefs all round it. Slightly to the west and north is situated Reuben Point, already mentioned, and one mile and three-quarters inside of this is the town of Lorenzo Marques. Within recent years great improvements have taken place here. On the occasion of my first visit the town was almost surrounded by a noisome fever-breeding swamp, which has since been remedied. English was scarcely understood, and lethargy was the distinguishing feature of the town. Owing to the infusion of fresh blood from the Cape Colony and Natal, new buildings soon began to overshadow the old flat-roofed Eastern ones, and the placidity of the streets was broken in upon by the appearance of waggons from the interior; new roads were laid down, and agencies from the leading commercial houses were established. The Portuguese, awaking to the importance of the place, re-buoyed the river and adopted a more liberal policy towards strangers.

Passing from the town, which has at the present time a population of about 2,000, we next come to the Berea, which is a low sandy ridge, covered with luxuriant foliage, amongst which the cocoa palms form a conspicuous feature. Some of these trees attain a height of sixty feet, and bear well. In this vicinity is situated a large and commodious hospital, capable of accommodating half the town; close to it is a trim little Roman Catholic Chapel. Turning eastward through some delightful foliage, we soon arrived at the quarters of the English and South African Telegraph Company, where the hospitable officials bade us welcome. The view of the town from this point is especially interesting, and while enjoying a rest in the commodious cantonment, I learned that the productions of the region are sugar-cane, indigo, pineapples, cocoa-nuts, orchilla weed, rice, maize, millet, tobacco, cereals, honey, bees-wax, dye woods, tortoise shell, amber, gum copal, india rubber, and a plentiful supply of Nature—hippopotamus, deer, leopards, lions, snakes, and others too numerous to mention. Insect life—owing to the moist nature of the climate—is extremely prolific, whilst flowers, for the same reason, abound in great variety. Indeed it would be hard to imagine a country better calculated to meet the views of the naturalist, botanist, and sportsman.

Looking westward and northward, a grand view of open water greets the eye. English River extends from Reuben Point for seven miles inland; in fact, there is room in this part of the harbour for thousands of ships of all tonnages. The Temby River is the southernmost of the tributaries of this inlet, which it joins about ten miles above the town. The steamship *Somtseu* has several times towed lighters forty miles up. It is about three-quarters of a mile wide at its junction with the English River, but about twenty miles up it narrows very considerably. The banks, for the most part, are lined with trees, and the country, though lying low, is open and beautiful; in places, extensive marshes occur, which are eminently suited for the production of rice. This river forms a waterway for the conveyance of machinery to the Swazie and Komatie Gold Fields, which are distant about 130 miles.

The climate of Delagoa Bay in winter is considerably hotter than that of Natal; but in summer, when the heavy rains prevail, the East African fever is apt to make its appearance. Care and temperance form the traveller's chief safeguards, but tourists and travellers are strongly recommended to choose the cooler and drier seasons. It must be borne in mind that, in these latitudes, midsummer occurs in December, and midwinter in June. The most desirable months are May, June, July, and August.

It would scarcely be fair to close a chapter on Delagoa Bay without especial mention of the natives, who differ entirely from those with whom we have already been brought into contact. They are, for the most part, members of the Amatonga tribe, and come from an independent territory, which is situated between the colony of Delagoa Bay and Zululand. These natives are not nearly so warlike as the Swazies or the Zulus; this is perhaps due to the relaxing nature of their climate and the prolonged association with the undesirable specimens of white adventurers who have for so long found a sanctuary in their territory. As a labourer, the Amatonga native is not to be surpassed; but he is not, in my opinion, to be very extensively trusted.

Before visiting the country of Amatongaland, something must be said touching the much-talked-about Delagoa Bay

The Union Steam Ship Company, Limited.

Railway. It will be remembered that, in the section dealing with the Transvaal Republic, President Burgers, in 1875, proceeded to Europe for the purpose of obtaining a loan of £300,000, with which to construct a railway from Delagoa Bay to Pretoria. The story of his failure has already been recorded in these pages. Another concession, in 1876, was entered into between the Portuguese Government and Mr. Moodie; the intention, in this case, being to form a company within six months to carry out the contract, which was to be completed within three years. The Transvaal Government, after paying Mr. Moodie the sum of £5,000 as honorarium and compensation, took over the contract. This was formed in Pretoria into a company, called "Lu Bomba Railway Company," with a capital of £110,000. Disaster, however, awaited this effort. Railway plant had been landed at Delagoa Bay, with the result of a loss of £5,598; shortly after this the Transvaal became a British Colony and the matter came to an end.

In the December of 1883, all previous concessions having lapsed, the Portuguese Government granted a new one to a company formed in London by Colonel McMurdo. The capital of this new venture was £500,000. The intention was to lay and work, under a concession for 99 years, a railway between Delagoa and the Transvaal, the Portuguese Government, meanwhile, being precluded from conceding or constituting any other railway to that Republic.

In June of 1887 the first sod was turned, and owing to the exertions of Sir Thomas Tancred, the first section of 55 miles was opened for traffic in November of the same year.

A further line, from Komatie Poort to Nels Spruit is now (1889) under consideration.

The kingdom of Amatongaland lies to the southward of Delagoa, and is bounded on the east by the Indian Ocean, on the west by Swazieland, and on the south by Zululand. The population is as yet a mere matter of conjecture, but it has been estimated at 85,000 to 90,000. The country is ruled over by a boy king, named Ungwanase, with Zambili, his mother, as regent. It is, for the most part, low-lying and unhealthy, except in winter. Game abounds, and owing to the warm and moist air, vegetation is luxuriant. The Amatongas have been frequently defeated by neighbouring tribes and their war-spirit knocked out of them. The best protection they have is to be found in the fever which, as I have said, at times prevails.

Sport is to be had in great variety, both in the rivers and woods; in short, the description of Delagoa Bay applies in almost every respect to this country. The natives, like the other African tribes, dress in a primitive sort of way, and the tourist, in preparing for a campaign in the land, will have to find out what kind of glass beads and trinkets are most acceptable at the time, as local tastes and fashions change as rapidly there as in civilised lands.

In my opinion, Amatongaland will be extremely useful to the Empire as a Native reserve, but in no other way. Owing to its position on the coast, and in view of the uncertainty that still over-hangs the future of Swazieland, it is imperative that the treaty entered into between Her Majesty's Government and the chiefs of Amatongaland should be upheld.

CHAPTER XXIII.

General Information—Routes to the Gold Fields.

HE Gold Fields of the Transvaal may be approached by a variety of routes, but the two most popular ones are viz.:—Cape Town via Kimberley to Johannesburg, Algoa Bay via Kimberley to Johannesburg.

There has been a considerable quantity of ink and energy wasted in advocating the several routes to it from the sea coast. The Cape Colony claims consideration owing to her long line of railway from Cape Town to Kimberley, and the fine mail-cart service between that port and the centre of attraction; while Natal boasts of a shorter and more direct route. The disadvantage of the Cape line is that the journey from Kimberley to Johannesburg is a night and day one, calculated to weary and exhaust the traveller, while on the other hand, the Natal route, though shorter by land and more comfortable in every respect, renders another 800 miles of sea voyage necessary. In my opinion, the two routes are about evenly balanced, the advantage, if any, lying on the Natal side; for a sea voyage in the well-appointed steamers now plying between the two ports means anything but hardship, while the rest of the journey is taken at leisure, accomplished in less time and passing through more enjoyable scenery. The costs of the routes are about equal. As regards convenience, those through the two English colonies are about on a par, though each colony, of course, claims for itself the advantage. The Delagoa Bay route, though necessitating the longest sea voyage, is by far the shortest land journey; but in summer, serious climatic drawbacks, together with the extreme roughness of the road and scanty accommodation, tell heavily against its popularity.

The Passenger fares from Delagoa Bay to the Komati are at present: 1st Class, 12s.; 2nd Class, 8s. 6d.; 3rd Class, 5s. From Barberton there is a regular service of Coaches to all Transvaal Centres.

The rates for Goods to the present terminus at Moveni are at present:

   £2 10s. per ton for ordinary goods.
   £3 10s. ,,   ,, hazardous goods.
    Terminal charges extra.

In the preceding chapters, full particulars of the several countries have been given, and a traveller may well be left to make his own selection.

The outfit suitable for an explorer or prospector will of course depend on what his intentions are. Should he intend to plunge into the western portions of the continent, Kimberley would be his point of departure. If to the north, or even east, it would be Pretoria. Having arrived at either of those centres, his first duty would be to provide himself with waggon, oxen, and men; these may be hired, but such a course is expensive, and not always satisfactory. His wisest course would be to consult some responsible citizen, and in those latitudes careful and experienced advice is always to be freely obtained, provided the traveller shows himself to be a decent man. The selection of a waggon is a most important task, as it will be his home for a considerable time. Especial attention should be paid to the wheels, which must be strong and of well seasoned wood. It is a good plan to have the tyres in segments, similar to the wheels of a field artillery gun; but when this is not possible, the metal should overhang the wood by a quarter of an inch. The axles should be examined for flaws, and attention paid to the bolts. The tool chest of the waggon should contain 3 gimlets, 2 augers, shifting spanner, 2 screw jacks, hammer, screws, nails, and waggon grease. The tent of the waggon should be of strong wooden bars, covered with an inner layer of painted canvas, and an outer of ordinary canvas. The inside fixings of the waggon should be two long box seats, running the entire length of the vehicle; these serve for provisions, clothes, trading truck, and books.

A good plan to lessen the jolt over rough roads is by fixing four carriage-springs inside the floor of the waggon and laying a false bottom on them. The hood may be covered inside with holland pockets into which a looking-glass, combs, brush, towels and spare every-day clothing, together with log-books, &c., may be put. Canvas flaps at either end, buttoning over well, transform the vehicle into a cosy chamber. I ought to have said that by this arrangement four companions may comfortably sleep in one waggon. Underneath the waggon, buckets and pots are suspended. Guns and revolvers ought to be fastened on the top of and inside the hood; these ought always to be clean and empty when put away. Some of the most terrible accidents have occurred by allowing weapons to lie about loose.

Draught cattle vary from £6 to £8 10s. per head. It is well to be sure that they have been inoculated against "lung sickness" and that they are not too old; before purchasing, a trial ought to be insisted on. As a rule, small Zulu oxen are the best, especially on the coast, for the following reasons:—They are less liable to sickness, they satisfy their hunger quicker, they are more enduring and not nearly so sullen as the heavier-built cattle of the uplands. Their disadvantages are a lack of bodily weight, rendering a greater number of them necessary, especially in crossing flooded rivers. The heavy or Dutch cattle are quite unsuited for the coast, but answer well on the great plains. Sixteen form a complete "span," though twelve would be quite enough to convey a ton or half-load anywhere

The waggon and cattle having been secured, their outfit next requires attention. The method of harnessing African teams is simple: a strong yoke is laid across the ox's neck and a couple of "wooden keys" put through holes in the yoke on either side of each ox's neck; a rheim or thong of hide with a running noose is next put over each beast's horns; the heads are then lashed together at a convenient distance, a neck-strap is now fastened to the keys under the ox's throat; by this means the yoke is brought to bear on the natural hump of the bullock. The yokes are then linked together by a chain at about nine feet interval. Of these rheims double sets ought to be provided: that is to say, two or even more for each ox, as they are liable to rot; and besides, should a wheel be broken, one of them soaked for a few hours in water and lashed firmly round the broken part will contract when dry and effectually remedy the damage. I have journeyed many hundred miles with such a splice.

Having thus acquired a waggon and oxen, attention is next called to the selection of men, of whom there must be at least three, viz.:—

First, a driver, who should be required to produce proof of his ability to guide a waggon over rough roads. On the wise selection of this man much of the success and pleasure of the journey will depend. Should he prove incompetent, cowardly or drunken, no end of trouble will be the result. There are always plenty of the right sort to be had. His wages range from 30s. to 60s. a month, and food.

The next is a lad whose duty it is to lead the cattle when on the march, to guide them into and out of dangerous places, and to herd them while grazing, as well as to be always at the beck and call of the driver, under whose command he is supposed to be. The wages of this lad range from 10s. to 20s. a month, and food. He is called a "forelouper."

The third is a cook, and may be another lad like the last, or a Parisian *chef*, just according to taste, though I would strongly prefer the savage. The wages of the cook are similar to those of the "forelouper." These three servants must be kept well in hand, otherwise they will take advantage. Any neglect of duty should be visited with swift punishment, which may take the form either of a fine, short rations, or a flogging.

For impertinence, I generally impose short rations—it touches the heart soonest; for dishonesty, flogging; and for neglect of duty, a fine. Once they realise that the "master" is neither a child nor a fool, they will settle down and be real treasures. On no pretence should liquors be given them. Familiarity or conversation should not be allowed to take place between them and the "master," who must be reserved and silent. Asking questions about the rivers, hills, roads or language of the country is not regarded as "conversation"—it is a part of their duty. Should one of these men get injured, nurse him kindly, but it is unwise to coddle or pamper him, as he is apt to develop chronic symptoms. Some of my men have received ghastly wounds, and after having them treated, have gone on with lighter duties, and in a day or so were restored. They recover much sooner than white men do. Anyone familiar with Africans will bear me out in this statement.

The times best suitable for travelling with cattle vary according to the state of the country and climate. On the great open plains in winter, day or night are alike to be used. Where the roads are bad, or where there are none, darkness must be avoided; but in hot localities good work is to be done in short two-hour "treks"; when the country is rough, early morning and often morning and evening "treks" are the best, thereby securing a long midday halt and feed for the cattle. Above all, long and weary marches are to be as far as possible avoided, as it expends too much vitality in one struggle, while no one can foretell what lies beyond the hills. "Reserve strength" is the African traveller's byword to success. It is wise to attend in a measure personally to the cattle, as the natives have little or no mercy on dumb beasts. Unless the leader of the expedition sees that they are properly watered, great tortures are likely to result. Carelessness on the part of the men in this department ought to be made a serious crime. I have on more than one occasion dismissed a man instantly, without wages, and in the wilds, for this offence. In crossing a drift (or ford) it is wise to take the cattle when they have been, say, an hour in yoke; they are warm to their work and not fagged—management and foresight are needed here. Should the waggon become wedged in a mud-hole, it is unwise to flog and yell at the oxen, as is the nature of the natives; strive by the exercise of a little ingenuity to release the wheels, with pick, shovel and screw-jack, then spur the cattle to it and man the wheels.

When cattle suffer from purging through change of grass or weather, administer a weak solution of alum (an oz. to the quart of water; give each sufferer one pint at once). When the reverse is the case, Epsom salts in a four-oz. dose will, as a rule, set matters right. It must be borne in mind that cattle are as subject to bowel disorders as men. Care should be taken in the wet season to camp and graze the cattle on heights, as in the valley they are apt to devour a weed called "tulip," which distends them and causes death in a few hours. The remedy for this is to relieve them by raking out the bowels by hand and administering a dose of one pound of the crushed roots of "tulip" in a quart of water, well boiled, and administered cold or nearly so. Care and attention to cattle is one of the traveller's prime duties.

Provisions.—The stock of food to be laid in depends on the nature and period of the journey. As a rule, it is well, when within the reach of civilisation, to take advantage of its comforts, and thereby husband the stock of tinned and preserved meats, &c., which may include potted beef and brawn, jams, pickles and fish, together with cornflour, bacon, sugar, coffee, tea, cocoa, condensed milk, baking-powder, flour, and salt. A good supply of plain biscuits is also of great service, as, owing to wet weather, it is often impossible to bake bread. Forestry tools, &c., in addition to scientific and photographic instruments; picks, shovels, axes, pestle, mortar and pan; nitric acid (1lb.), sulphuric acid (1lb.), wash-bowls, plates, cups, knives, forks, spoons. &c., are some of the main necessaries that occur to me. There are a host of other odds and ends which the traveller, according as his station or his tastes may dictate.

The Medicines which, in ten years of constant travel, I have found most useful are—sweet oil and liquid ammonia for making hartshorn, for bruises, sprains and lumbago; Eno's fruit salt, acetic acid, antibilious pills, chlorodyne, laudanum, eau-de-luce, and permanganate of potash (for snake-bites); collodion, lint, and sticking-plaster for wounds; Epsom salts and alum for cattle.

In cases of sickness amongst the men, the following simple remedies are useful:—

Dysentery.—Change of diet to cornflour; in acute cases, laudanum and castor oil in small doses. Keep the abdomen and kidneys warm; avoid highly-seasoned foods, liquors, or fatigue.

Fever.—Strip the patient and rub into his spine a diluted solution of acetic acid. Wrap up warmly. Keep the bowels open by mild aperient. Avoid highly-seasoned food. Game, meat soup, Liebig's extract and other nourishing articles may be administered. Interest him in something, and free his mind from dread.

An Open Flesh Wound.—In ordinary cases, soak lint in collodion and apply bandage of clean linen, taking care to bring the lips of the wound together.

Ulcers are one of the most painful evils of African travel. When large and open with dark blue rings of inflammation, bathe in hot water, until all pus is removed. Test for proud flesh; if any, burn it out with alum or caustic; then bathe, and mix honey and flour in equal parts, and apply as a salve. No intoxicating liquor of any kind should be taken, and the bowels must be kept in good order. Where ulcers occur, as a rule the patient is proof against the Coast fever.

I might go on for pages multiplying examples of treatment, but each traveller must pick up and apply his own experience. Snake-bites are extremely rare, but when they do occur, prompt measures are advisable, as follows: stop the poison-flow by a bandage, into which a stone, a tobacco-pipe or any thing else solid, may be put, over the artery; then twist firmly, administer twenty drops of eau-de-luce every hour, and cauterise the wound by opening it with a lancet or knife, and rubbing in nitrate of silver or eau-de-luce. Where surgical knowledge is possessed, a sub-cutaneous injection of permanganate of potash is a certain cure, but care is necessary here, as other evils may be caused. Give the patient brandy—make him half-drunk in fact, and keep him excited, by arguments about different kinds of snakes. Assert that the one that bit him was not poisonous. Any one possessing an intimate knowledge of human nature, is acquainted with the fact that, in such cases, a morbid imagination will do as much to kill the sufferer as the poison itself.

Fuel in certain parts of Africa is a great difficulty; sometimes for hundreds of miles there is not a tree or even a twig to be seen. In such cases cattle and game droppings is a good substitute. Let the forelouper and cook carry bags to collect scraps while en route and always keep about a hundredweight in stock, for when it rains the traveller, if he has none in stock and dry, is apt to be in a sad plight.

When a side journey is desired it is advisable to employ, when possible, a native of the district as guide, but enquiries should always be made as to the condition of the tribes. These bearers generally cost one shilling a day and food, which like that of the expeditionary men, consists of Indian meal and salt. Now and then broad and flooded rivers have to be crossed. When the depth of water is too great to allow of fording it on foot, a handy and serviceable raft may be constructed by lashing bundles of dry reeds together with bark rope, until a raft thirty feet by fifteen feet is constructed; this ought to be wedge-shaped and thin at the point. By strengthening it with saplings and curving the bows upward by means of rope made of bark, a safe boat capable of carrying half a ton is produced. When necessary to send it with stores to a party on the further bank, it will float across on the kite principle if properly managed. A very slight knowledge of emchanics is necessary here.

R.M.S. "TARTAR," 4,246 Tons, 4,900 H.P.

CHAPTER XXIV.

How to get to SOUTH AFRICA—Outfit—History of the UNION STEAM SHIP COMPANY.

UNCERTAINTY OF PAST TIMES REMOVED—FACILITIES FOR INFORMATION—OUTFIT—SAFETY OF OCEAN VOYAGES COMPARED TO RAILWAY TRAIN TRAVELLING—HISTORY OF THE UNION STEAM SHIP COMPANY—LIST OF FLEET AND TONNAGE—RECORDS OF SPEED—THE SERVICES—THE VOYAGE TO THE CAPE—GENERAL INFORMATION FOR PASSENGERS.

UNTIL very recent times, the scarcity of authentic and reliable descriptions and Guides to our South African Dominions has proved a serious barrier to the popularity of those most interesting and promising regions. A dread and uncertainty overhung the land; and, as a consequence, none but daring and experienced travellers cared to undertake the journey to it. Such, however, is no longer the case, for once the decision is arrived at to visit or settle in the South African Colonies, ample instructions are available, and at a price which brings them within the reach of the most impecunious.

Owing to the rapid commercial development of South Africa within the past thirty years, steam communication on the most approved principles has been established between England, Cape Town, and the adjacent ports on the South and East Coasts of the African Continent. The intending voyager having satisfied himself as to the speed, accommodation and fares of the vessels which link the two countries, finds his next difficulty in the selection of outfit; and here it is that serious blunders are oftentimes made. Clothing of the lightest description is erroneously considered an essential, whereas a usual English outfit is absolutely necessary, especially if the traveller proposes to visit the uplands of the country in the vicinity of the Diamond and Gold Fields, where the temperature is often particularly cold.

It must be borne in mind that a great climatic difference exists between South Africa and those portions of East Africa which have been brought prominently forward in recent works of Exploration. Instead of falling into this mistake, let the outfit comprise warm under-flannels, lambs-wool socks, and strong plain tweed outer garments; a very few articles of a gauzy nature, for exceptionally hot days, may be added as matters of luxury. The exact nature of an outfit cannot, of course, be laid down here; but let each one, according to his or her means, provide against cold winds and wet weather.

If the course of travel is likely to lie in the civilised parts of the country, a large selection of clothing is not absolutely necessary, as one can obtain anything (but a good fit) in the Colonies. The outfit purchased and passage secured (full directions for which see elsewhere in this volume), the traveller may resign himself to the tender mercies of the high seas in full confidence, for the stout, strong and well-found ships are less liable, by 50 per cent., to accident, disaster and wreckage than an ordinary railway train. The few isolated cases of shipwreck are always, owing to exhaustive Courts of Inquiry, brought out in strong relief; but a reference to the number of safe and prosperous voyages made by vessels of the Union Steam Ship Company will serve to re-assure the mind of even the most timid and fearful.

While on this subject, a slight reference to the history and services of this Company may prove interesting; for the line, as will be seen, has played no unimportant part in the revolution which has taken place in the affairs of British South Africa.

In 1853 the Company first appeared (floated, so to speak, in both senses), with a small fleet of five steamers as follows:— *The Briton*, 491 tons; *The Dane* and *The Norman*, 530 tons each; *The Saxon*, 440 tons, and *The Union*, 336 tons.

It was not until the outbreak of the Crimean War, however, that the line became recognised as one of national importance. Owing to the pressure on the steam resources of the nation,

The Union Steam Ship Company, Limited.

the Company found it necessary to add to their fleet another and a larger vessel, *i.e.*, *The Celt*, 585 tons.

At the close of the war the Company underwent enlargement and assumed its present style and title.

The year 1857 proved a most eventful one in the history of the enterprise, for then it was that the first contract was entered upon between Her Majesty's Government and the Line, for the conveyance of Mails between the Cape of Good Hope and England.

The *Dane* was the first steamer to set out on this new and important Imperial task. She was followed shortly after by the *Celt* and the *Norman*, after which the voyages were undertaken at regular monthly intervals.

The necessity for larger vessels now became apparent, and the *Phœbe* and *Athens* were added to the fleet. This was followed by still further additions in 1860. The *Cambrian*, 1,054 tons, and the *Briton*, of 1,116 tons, to replace the smaller vessel, which was sold; and in 1862 the *Roman* and the *Saxon*, each of 1,200 tons. (The *Roman* was afterwards enlarged to 1,850 tons.)

During the next five years the service was conducted on such satisfactory lines, as to induce the Government at the expiration of that period to invite tenders from the Company for a second contract, which was entered upon. Meanwhile ocean postal communication between the Cape and Natal (810 miles further north), had been carried on by the Company under an agreement with the Natal Government since 1st October, 1865. In order to meet the requirements of this extension, the Directors provided a light-draft steam ship suitable for crossing the harbour bar at Port Natal.

In 1864, the operations of the Company were extended to Mauritius under contracts with the Government of that island. This year marked the increase of the fleet by two new vessels, in order to meet the increasing trade and importance of the regions. A bi-monthly service between England and the Cape was established, and the capital of the Company increased to £260,000, with power to increase still further.

In May, 1865, the first disaster occurred when the *Athens* was lost in Table Bay; most of the vessels in port at that time were dashed ashore; while the terrible hurricane that raged at that time along the African coast, is to this day remembered and spoken of with awe.

In 1867 a semi-monthly Mail service was established between the Cape of Good Hope and England, and the terms of the Governmental Contract increased.

For several years the Company's operations continued without any noticeable event, saving the continued activity of all concerned in the efforts to meet the constantly increasing requirements of the trade.

The next important movement in connection with the Company's operations, was that which excited so much parliamentary controversy in 1873, the main features of which were as follows:—A contract was entered into between the Company and H.M.'s Government:—1st. For an extension of Postal Service, on the main line, by three departures monthly, instead of two each way, and a reduction of the contract time from 37 to 30 days, exclusive of stoppages; and 2nd. A new Service every four weeks between Cape Town and Zanzibar. These enlarged operations required the provision of six new steam ships at a cost of £256,000, and an additional £150,000 for renovating the largest and best vessels of the Company's existing fleet, and supplying them with new and more powerful engines on the compound principle. As soon as the arrangements were concluded with the Government, the Directors set to work to make the necessary preparations by the acquisition of new steam ships; and at the beginning of the year, dependent on the faith of the House of Commons to ratify the Government contract, the running of three steamers monthly was commenced.

The strong opposition which was got up in the House of Commons, however, resulted in the withdrawal of the new contract, and the revival of the one then existing, which continued in force till June, 1876.

The Union Steam Ship Company, Limited.

The Zanzibar contract was finally settled at £20,000 per annum for eight years.

Notwithstanding the adverse result to the interests of the Union Company consequent on the abandonment of a contract, on the faith of which they had expended such a large sum of money, the Company loyally carried out their intentions and thereby gave the Colonists and merchants the full benefit of three Mail services per month in lieu of two; and although working under a contract, which allowed them 37 days for the voyage, their steamers regularly performed the voyage in ten or twelve days less than the stipulated time.

The heavy expenditure caused by the extended preparations, and the unexpected withdrawal of the additional Postal receipts, prevented the payment of any dividend for the year 1874. It is reasonably to be hoped that such an untoward event will never again occur in the history of the Company.

In October, 1876, a new seven years' contract was entered upon with the Cape of Good Hope Government (who were represented by the Crown Agents for the Colonies) for a fortnightly service between Plymouth and Table Bay, and *vice versâ*, the length of voyage not to exceed twenty-six days, except when the Islands of St. Helena or Ascension were called at, for which call an additional day was allowed. This contract carried with it no subsidy, the payment being by the postage on the Mails, and certain fixed premiums for increased speed. In 1879, the Company, in view of the heavy pressure on the Transport Department of the Admiralty, owing to the Zulu War, placed the *Asiatic*, the *Teuton*, and the *American* at the service of the Government.

Of these vessels the two former were despatched; the *Asiatic*, with 281 officers and men, and 112 women and children, and the *Teuton*, with 605 officers and men on board; whilst the *American*, in addition to her passengers, carried 423 officers and men; making a total of 1,309 officers and men and 112 women and children.

On receipt of the news of the disaster at Isandula, this

Company again rendered good service by conveying troops to the seat of war with promptitude.

The R.M.S. *Pretoria* was selected by the Government for this purpose, and after being fitted out with astonishing dispatch and inspected by H.S.H. Prince Edward, set out on her voyage of rescue—on the 20th February—and in 24 days and 8 hours, including stoppages, landed her freight of 942 soldiers in safety. Not only was she the first to leave with the called-for reinforcements, but she achieved the fastest passage on record.

At the same time a further detachment of officers and men of the 60th Rifles, 219 in number, together with the late Prince Imperial and suite, set out for Natal in the *Danube*, where they arrived in safety.

On the 23rd April, 1880, the *American*, when two degrees north of the equator, on her outward voyage, broke her mainshaft in a most unusual and inconvenient place. The violent revolutions of the engines caused a serious fracture in the machinery; and in spite of great exertions on the part of the passengers, officers and crew, it was found impossible to resume the voyage. All hands, however, escaped in safety, one life being lost afterwards, but not in a Union boat. (For full account, see *Historical Sketch of the Union Company*.)

In March, 1880, H.I.M. the Empress Eugenie set out to view the death place of the lamented Prince who had fallen in the Zulu War, and arrangements having been made, she embarked with her suite on R.M.S. *German* on the 25th March, and landed at Natal on the 23rd of the next month. Her Majesty, together with her suite, expressed themselves as most gratified with the accommodation and attention which they had enjoyed.

In April, 1885, when there appeared every probability of an outbreak of hostilities between this country and Russia, and when the Admiralty were desirous of placing fast merchant steamers as armed cruisers at various Colonial ports for the

The Union Steam Ship Company, Limited.

protection of coaling stations, &c., two of the Union Company's Mail steamers were selected to act in defence of the South African Colonies. The *Moor*, then on her way out to the Cape of Good Hope, and the *Mexican*, at Southampton, were chartered for this service, the former vessel being ordered by cable to Simon's Bay to be fitted, whilst the *Mexican* was specially despatched from Southampton at short notice for the same purpose. Only the *Moor*, however, was actually commissioned as an armed cruiser, she being supplied with an armament of six guns and a crew of 110 officers and men, principally members of the Royal Naval Reserve. She was taken on a cruise up the East Coast of Africa, under the orders of the Commander-in-Chief on the station, Rear-Admiral Sir Walter J. Hunt-Grubbe, K.C.B., and was the only merchant vessel which actually armed and hoisted the pennant or was commissioned under the command of a naval officer. The *Mexican* was employed as a transport, and conveyed troops from Cape Town to Hong-Kong and thence to England.

By way of conclusion to this sketch of the history of the Union Company, and as a contrast to the diminutive fleet of 1854, previously described, a list of the Company's present steamers is appended, viz.:—

NAME.	TONS.	H.P.
1. MEXICAN	4,549	4,600
2. TARTAR	4,246	4,900
3. ATHENIAN	3,782	4,600
4. MOOR	3,597	4,500
5. TROJAN	3,471	4,100
6. SPARTAN	3,403	4,100
7. PRETORIA	3,198	3,650
8. ARAB	3,145	3,000
9. NUBIAN	2,998	1,800
10. GERMAN	3,007	2,650
11. DURBAN	2,808	2,800
Carry over	38,204	40,700

NAME.	TONS.	H.P.
Brought forward	38,204	40,700
12. ANGLIAN ...	2,245 ...	1,700
13. ROMAN ...	1,750 ...	1,200
14. AFRICAN	1,372 ...	1,300
15. TYRIAN (building)	1,540 ...	1,100
16. NORSEMAN do.	930	700
17. SAXON ...	468 ...	500
18. UNION	113 ...	300
19. CARNARVON	103 ...	200
TOTAL	46,725	47,700

All of these are fitted with tri-compound engines except the *Nubian, German, Durban* and *Roman,* which have the compound 2-cylinder engines.

The following is a List of the Fastest Passages made in the Cape of Good Hope Mail Service by the Union Steam Ship Company's Royal Mail Steamers. These voyages were made between Plymouth and Cape Town, and *vice versâ,* and the net steaming time on such passages is given as the most reliable basis for comparison:—

SHIP.	OUT. DYS. HRS.	SHIP.	HOME. DYS. HRS.
MEXICAN ...	18 1	TARTAR	17 1
ATHENIAN	18 6	ATHENIAN ...	17 4
MOOR	18 10	MEXICAN ...	17 21
PRETORIA ...	18 11	MOOR	17 21
TARTAR	18 14	DURBAN	18 2
DURBAN	18 16	PRETORIA ...	18 5
TROJAN	19 0	ARAB	18 5
SPARTAN ...	19 1	TROJAN	18 12
GERMAN ...	19 6	SPARTAN ...	18 17
ARAB	19 11	GERMAN	18 21

The voyages are now made between Southampton and Cape Town and *vice versâ.*

The Union Steam Ship Company, Limited.

THE SERVICES NOW PERFORMED BY THE UNION COMPANY

are—

1st. The Cape of Good Hope Mail Service.

2nd. The Natal Mail Service.

3rd. The Continental and Intermediate Service.

Cape Mail Service.—The Royal Mail Steamers leave Southampton, under contract with the Cape of Good Hope Government, every alternate Friday. Homewards, the packets leave Cape Town every alternate Wednesday. The time occupied between Southampton and Cape Town and *vice versâ* is about $19\frac{1}{2}$ days.

The Natal Mail Service.—The steamers performing the Cape Mail Service convey the Natal Mails between Southampton and Cape Town and *vice versâ*, transhipping them to and receiving them from Intercolonial steamers at the latter port. The steamer for Natal leaves Cape Town immediately after the arrival of the ocean steamer from England, and the Homeward steamer from Natal leaves that port on the Thursday preceding the departure from Cape Town of the Mail steamer for England.

Continental and Intermediate Service.—The Steamers in this Service leave Hamburg, Rotterdam and Southampton monthly; and additional Steamers are despatched from Southampton direct, making, with the Mail Steamers, a Weekly Service from England. In addition to the through steamer from Hamburg and Rotterdam a Branch Steamer from Hamburg and Antwerp connects with each alternate Mail Steamer.

GENERAL INFORMATION TO PASSENGERS.

The voyage to the Cape has been described by so many writers that any extended reference to it here would be superfluous. It has, and with truth, been called "the most delightful voyage in the world." After the Bay of Biscay, with its chronic "lumpiness," is passed, the skies assume a more limpid blue, the water a richer tint, while the balmy airs that sweep the deck proclaim—

> That the piercing winds and the whirling snow

have been left behind. The glimpses afforded of the islands are pleasant interludes to the regular and well-ordered life of the ship, while each day presents its own panorama of tinted clouds and of sunlit sea.

The Rates of Passage Money, by the UNION LINE, to South Africa, are moderate; those by Intermediate Steamers being rather less than by the Mail Steamers. The Passage Money, in every case, covers all requisites for the voyage, and includes free Railway conveyance from London to Southampton or from Plymouth to Southampton. Passengers can leave London on the morning of sailing, and embark in comfort at Southampton, the short journey enabling their friends to accompany them and return again to London the same afternoon. Friends of Passengers are, by a special arrangement between the UNION COMPANY and the London and South-Western Railway Company, allowed to travel to Southampton and back at the Single Journey Fare. The Steamers of the UNION LINE are provided with every comfort and modern improvement, the Electric Light and Refrigerators being fitted in all the Mail Steamers. A qualified Surgeon is carried on board each Steamer, and experienced Stewardesses are also at the service of lady Passengers. Handbook of Information containing all details, Fares, &c., will be sent on application to the UNION STEAM SHIP COMPANY, 11, Leadenhall Street, London; or to any of the AGENTS of the Company named on Pages 212 to 215.

APPENDICES.

List of Native Words and Phrases.

English.	Native.	English.	Native.
Man	Indoda or Umuntu	Foam	Kihliza
Young Man	Insizwa	Mist	Inkungu
Boy	Umfana	Rain	Imvula
Woman or Wife	Umfasie	Fire	Umlilo
Grown Girl	Intombie	Smoke	Intutu
Young Girl	Intombazana	Fowl	Inkuku
Child	Umtwana	Eggs	Amaquanda
Head	Ikanda	Beef	Inyama
Body	Umzimba	Fish	Inhlanzi
Arm	Ingalo	Worms	Insundu
Leg	Umlenzi	Paper	Ikasi
Foot	Inyonw	Stick	Induku or Uti
Hand	Isandhla	Firewood	Izinkoonie
Finger	U'Moonwaa	Pot	Embeesa or Totosa
Eye	Iliso	Spoon	E'kesa
Mouth	Umlomo	Knife	Mūkwa
Teeth	Mazinyah	Sour Milk	A'Maas
Hair	N'wellie	Corn (Indian)	Umbilo
Abdomen	Seeswa	Give	Nika
Skin	Skoomba	Go	Hamba
Water	A'manzie	Get out	Pooma
River	Umfula	Quick	Teh-Teha

List of Native Words and Phrases—*continued*

English.	Native.	English.	Native.
Come	Eza	Silence	Tula
See	Bona	Speak	Kuluma
Good	Lŭngili	Pull	Donsa
Nice to look at	Inhla	Wade	Wella
Nice to taste	Manandie	Drink	Puza
Hammer	Kanda	To Smoke	Bema
Strike	Tyaya	To Rest	Pumulo
Run	Kejima	Chief or King	Inkosi
Stop	Nyatella	"Your Majesty"	Byatu
Throw	Ponsa	Chieftain	Induna
Catch or Hold	Bamba	Queen	Inkosigazie
Grind	Gia	Great	Inkulu
Lift	Pagameesa	Mountain	Intaba
Carry	Twala	Far	Koodie
Listen	Lalela	Hole	Embobo or Umkodi
Year	Inyaka		
Month	Inyanga	To Stab	Kwaza
Moon	,,	Love	Tanda
Day	Nsuku	Want	Fuua
Morning	Kusasa	I	Mena
Midday	Imini	You	Wena
Afternoon	M'tambama	The Heavens	E'zulu
Evening	Ukuthewa	The Tribe	Ama-zulu
Darkness	Busuku	Yes	Yebo
Sleep	Ubutongu	No	Kabo
Lie down	Lelapanzi	Shoes or Sandals	Iziskatula
Arise	Vuka	To Dream	Pupa
Call	Beza	A Dwelling	Indhlu

The Union Steam Ship Company, Limited.

List of Native Words and Phrases—*continued*.

English.	Native.	English.	Native.
A Village	Mooze	Marriage	U'Kuzeka
One	Munya	Path	Endhlela
Two	Mabeelie	Dog	Inja
Three	Matatu	Sin	Sona
Four	Manie	Carry	Twala
Five	Shlanu	Birth	Zala
Six	Setupa	Go	E'ah
Seven	Isikombesa	Light	U'Lula
Eight	Sheeagalwo-Umbeelie	Blanket	Ingubu
		Beads	U'Buthalo
Nine	Sheeagaho-Munya	Shelter	Seteesa
		Cook	Pega
Ten	Shumie	Food	Guthla
Prophet	Inyanga	My	Wami
Prophetess	Sangome	Look	Bega
Witch or Wizard	Umtagati	Money	Mali
Flowers	Mabalana	Dig	Imba
Many	Maningi	A Fence	Etangu
To Call	Beza	Gardens	Enseemu
Cattle	Inkomo	To Hoe	Lema
Do not	Unga	A Hoe	Egaja
Make	Enza	A Girdle	Mutcha
Bird	Inyoni	Fight	Elwa
A Lion	Um bube	Kill	Bulala
Wolf	Empeece	Eat	Ethla
Jackall	M'Kanshan	To Bath	Bugutu
Deer or Game	Inyamazana	Wash	Gaza
Serpent	Inyoka	To Sink	Shona
A Name	Egama	A Horse	Ehash

List of Native Words and Phrases—*continued.*

English.	Native.	English.	Native.
Donkey	Bungolo	To Stand	Ema
Seat	Ehlalo	To Run	Ke jima
To Sit	Shalo	A Basket	Imbeugi

Phrases.

English.	Native.
Inquire who is there.	Buza weto obani lapa na.
What do you want?	Funani na?
Call the men	Bezanie amadoda.
Give me my shoes	Niga Iziskatula wami.
Saddle the horse	Bopela ehash.
Water the horse	Puzesa ehash.
Is it far?	Goodie eny na?
Is your King here?	Inkosi wako Kona lapo na?
The King is not here to-day	Inkosi agako numthla.
Go like men and not cowards	Hambanie, fanaka amadoda, ungu fanaka ama gwala.
I will come to-morrow	Ge aza ungumusa.
Inspan the cattle	Bopela izinkabie.
Outspan the cattle	Kumulo izinkabie.
Do not make a noise	Unga banga umsendo.
Go quickly	Hamba na-majuban.
Gently, not too fast	Gathlie.
Pull together, men	Dousa ganya madoda.
Grind corn	Gia umbela.
Give me water	Nigela amanzie.

The Union Steam Ship Company, Limited.

Phrases—continued.

English.	Native.
Light the fire	Vutela umlela.
Put out the fire	Cima umlela.
Kill a fowl	Bulala inkuku.
Pluck it	Thluta izimpape.
Wake me early	Vusela kusasa-u-kusain.
At sunrise	Ka puma elanga.
Give me my rifle	Nigezella, sebam samie ka inhlamvu.
Give me my shot gun	Nigezella, sebam samie ka-tehlwi.
Is the river deep?	Umfalu ya shona na.
How is the bottom?	Enjani aka panziena?
Stones or rocks only?	A matcha odwana?

The above are spelled as nearly phonetically as possible.

LATITUDES AND LONGITUDES.

Place.	Latitude.		Longitude.	
	Deg.	Min.	Deg.	Min.
Outer anchorage, Natal	29	53	31	4
Durban, Port Natal	29	52	31	0
Pietermaritzburg	29	35	30	23
Greytown	29	3	30	35
Harrismith, O.F.S.	28	16	29	5
Potchefstroom, O.F.S.	26	43	27	33
Pretoria, Transvaal	25	44	28	25
Great Usutu Drift, Swaziland	26	47	31	7
Dideen, Royal Kraal, Swaziland	26	34	31	20
Crossing of White Umbeloosi, Swaziland	26	27	31	25
Umbeloosi Poort (Slavers)	26	15	31	56
Lorenzo Marques, Delagoa Bay	25	.58	32	37

ALTITUDES.

CAPE COLONY.—Grahamstown, 1,700 feet; Bedford, 2,500; Cradock, 3,000; Middelburg, 4,200; Colesberg, 4,730.

ORANGE FREE STATE.—Bethulie, 4,400 feet; Philopolis, 4,600; Fauresmith, 4,800; Bethany, 4,600; Bloemfontein, 4,750; Fountain Valley, near Bloemfontein, 4,770; Thaba N'Chu, 5,250.

GRIQUALAND WEST.—Kimberley, 4,400 feet; Christiana, 4,250; Pokwane Gasibone's Town, 4,200.

TRANSVAAL.—Bloemhof, 4,450 feet; Pretoria, 4,620; Potchefstroom, 4,780; Witwater Rand, 4,930; Standerton, 5,200; Heidelberg, 5,400; Wakkerstroom, 6,000; Utrecht, 4,300.

NATAL.—Maritzburg, 2,000 feet; Colenso, 3,320; Howick, 3,700; Estcourt, 3,900; Newcastle 4,100; The Plains (Harding's Store), 5,200.

WEATHER SIGNS.

A very clear sunset of pale gold is a sign of fine weather, if with a calm and dewy evening.

A clear orange sunset foretells a very fine day, and more surely if with a rising barometer and calm, dewy evening.

A clear sky, and sun setting in a well-defined form, without dazzling the eye, and of a deep salmon, foreshadows a brilliant and a very hot day to succeed.

The same appearance, with a cream haze on horizon, is also a sign of fine hot weather; but in this case the sun becomes deeper just before he disappears.

The same appearance at sunset in winter is attended by the sharpest frost of the season.

If in unsettled weather the wind veers from S.W. to W. or N.W. at sunset, expect fine weather for a day or two.

In showery seasons, and when a day finer than before, if the wind returns again from W. or N.W. to S. or S.S.E. at sunset, be sure of a return of rain and storm.

At any season the barometer will rise while the wind works from S. to W. and N.W., and will fall while it recedes from westward to southward, a good rule whereby to judge of what is near both in summer and winter.

TABLE OF DISTANCES BETWEEN DURBAN AND THE TRANSVAAL GOLD FIELDS BY WAGGON ROAD.

From Durban to—	Miles.	Yards
Pietermaritzburg	57	—
Greytown	42	—
Burrup's	9	23
Mooi River	14	1,083
Tugela River	12	240
Sand Spruit	16	626
Helpmakaar	11	485
Dundee (Still's)	22	1,200
Lantman's, Buffalo River	10	500
De Jager's, Buffalo River Drift	7	1,004
Blood River	17	1,477

TABLE OF DISTANCES—*continued.*

From Durban to—	Miles.	Yards.
Umvoloosi River	11	1,136
Umpemfaau River	11	1,065
Pongola River	28	225
Umkoyan River	7	1,685
Mugan River	7	380
Assegai River	8	1,276
Derby	18	1,379
Thello River	5	1,374
Imquampisi River	16	1,128
Amsterdam		—
Usutu River	11	600
Impuluse River	19	479
Junction with Lake Chrissie Road	17	—
Hot Springs	17	1,204
Koma'i River	7	27
Top White Hill	12	918
Top Red Hill	3	640
Foot of the Berg	13	1,540
Queen's River	13	1,400
Lower Camp, Moodie's	4	—
Whole distance	363	214

TABLE OF DISTANCES BETWEEN PORTS.

ATLANTIC DISTANCES.

SOUTHAMPTON.							
133	PLYMOUTH.						
862	768	LISBON.					
1306	1212	546	MADEIRA.				
1517	1422	708	253	TENERIFFE.			
1537	1442	710	282	45	LAS PALMAS.		
4848	4254	3509	3042	2737	2705	ST. HELENA	
5979	5885	5113	4673	4426	4413	1695	CAPE TOWN.

CAPE TOWN.			
1695	ST. HELENA.		
2395	700	ASCENSION.	
4673	3042	2466	MADEIRA.

COAST DISTANCES.

SOUTH AFRICA.

CAPE TOWN.							
250	MOSSEL BAY.						
297	52	KNYSNA.					
440	199	150	ALGOA BAY.				
496	252	203	68	KOWIE.			
560	320	268	135	65	E. LONDON.		
810	580	528	395	325	260	NATAL.	
1120	900	848	705	635	570	310	DELAGOA BAY.

TABLE OF DISTANCES

OF

The Principal South African Towns from the Nearest Ports.

N.B.—This Table has been compiled from the most reliable sources, but its correctness cannot be guaranteed.

Town.	Nearest Port.	Distance.	Means of Conveyance.
Aberdeen	Algoa Bay	166 miles	145 miles by Rail to Aberdeen Road.
Alexandria	Algoa Bay	58 ,,	
Algoa Bay, or Port Elizabeth			
Alice	East London	84 ,,	42 miles by Rail, Eastern System to King William's Town.
Aliwal, North	East London	280 ,,	Rail, Eastern System.
Aliwal, South, or Mossel Bay			
Balfour	East London	132 ,,	42 miles by Rail to King William's Town.
Barberton			
Barkly	Cape Town	669 ,,	
,,	Algoa Bay	507 ,,	
Bathurst	Port Alfred	10 ,,	
Beaufort, Fort	East London	102 ,,	42 miles by Rail to King William's Town.
Beaufort, West	Cape Town	339 ,,	Rail, Western System.
Bedford	Algoa Bay	151 ,,	127 miles by Rail, Midland System to Cookhouse.
Blanco	Mossel Bay	18 ,,	
Bloemfontein	Cape Town	776 ,,	608 miles by Rail from Colesberg, via De Aar Junction.
,,	Algoa Bay	477 ,,	308 miles by Rail from Colesberg.
Burghersdorp	East London	244 ,,	Rail, Eastern System.
Caledon	Cape Town	63 ,,	
Cathcart	East London	109 ,,	Rail, Eastern System.
Cape Town			
Ceres	Cape Town	94 ,,	85 miles by Rail to Ceres Road, Western System.
Claremont	Cape Town	6½ ,,	Rail, Western System.
Colesberg	Algoa Bay	308 ,,	Rail, Midland System.
Cookhouse	Algoa Bay	127 ,,	Rail, Midland System.
Cradock	Algoa Bay	182 ,,	Rail, Midland System.

The Union Steam Ship Company, Limited.

Town.	Nearest Port.	Distance.	Means of Conveyance.
De Aar Junction	Cape Town	501 miles	Rail, Western System.
De Aar Junction	Algoa Bay	339 "	Rail, Midland System.
Diamond Fields (Kimberley)	Cape Town	647 "	Rail.
	Algoa Bay	485 "	Rail.
Dordrecht	East London	250 "	154 miles by Rail to Queenstown.
Drakenstein	Cape Town	36 "	
Durban	Natal		
East London			
Fauresmith	Algoa Bay	477 "	308 miles by Rail, Midland System, to Colesberg.
Fransche Hoek	Cape Town	60 "	
Frasersberg	Cape Town	360 "	Rail to Frasersberg Road, 290 miles.
George	Mossel Bay	22 "	
Graaff Reinet	Algoa Bay	185 "	Rail, Midland System.
Grahamstown	Port Alfred	42 "	Rail.
"	Algoa Bay	106 "	Rail.
Hanover	Algoa Bay	355 "	300 miles to Hanover Road by Rail, Midland System.
"	Cape Town	547 "	539 miles to Hanover Road by Rail, Western System.
Harrismith	Durban	210 "	
Heidelberg	Mossel Bay	76 "	
Hopetown	Algoa Bay	"	Rail from Orange River, 408 miles.
"	Cape Town	"	Rail from Orange River, 570 miles.
Humansdorp	Algoa Bay	80 "	
Jansenville	Algoa Bay	147 "	
Johnanesburg			
Kalk Bay	Cape Town	17 "	Rail, Western System.
Kimberley	Diamond Fields		
King Williamstown	East London	42 "	Rail, Eastern System.
Klip Drift	Algoa Bay	445 "	
Knysna	Mossel Bay	82 "	
Ladysmith	Durban	130 "	
Leydenburg	Durban	385 "	
Malmesbury	Cape Town	49 "	Rail, Western System.
Maritzburg	(See Pietermaritzburg.)	70 "	Rail, Natal Government System.
Middleburg	Algoa Bay	250 "	243 miles by Rail, Midland System.
Mossel Bay			

P

Town.	Nearest Port.	Distance.	Means of Conveyance.
Murraysburg...	Cape Town	517 miles	404 miles by Rail from Biejespoort, Western System.
,, ...	Algoa Bay	251 ,,	185 miles by Rail to Graaff Reinet, Midland System.
Natal ...			
Oudtshoorn ...	Mossel Bay	57 ,,	
Paarl ...	Cape Town	36 ,,	Rail, Western System.
Panmure, or East London ...			
Peddie ...	Algoa Bay	173 ,,	Rail to Grahamstown.
Pietermaritzburg ...	Durban ...	70 ,,	Rail.
Port Elizabeth ...			
Port Alfred, or the Kowie ...			
Port Nolloth ...	Cape Town	300 ,,	Steamer.
Potchefstroom ...	Durban ...	420 ,,	
Pretoria ...	Durban ...	380 ,,	
Prince Albert ...	Mossel Bay	132 ,,	
	Cape Town	295 ,,	265 miles by Rail to Prince Albert Road.
Queenstown ...	East London	154 ,,	Rail, Eastern System.
Richmond ...	Algoa Bay	293 ,,	243 miles by Rail, Midland System to Middleburg Road.
Riversdale ...	Mossel Bay	45 ,,	
Robertson ...	Cape Town	145 ,,	
Saldanha Bay ...	Cape Town	80 ,,	Sea.
Simon's Bay ...	Cape Town	23 ,,	Rail to Kalk Bay (Wynberg Line), thence by Passenger cart (6 miles)
Somerset, East	Algoa Bay	140 ,,	Rail, Midland System to Cookhouse.
Somerset, West	Cape Town	30 ,,	
Stellenbosch...	Cape Town	31 ,,	Rail, Western System.
Stockenstroem	Algoa Bay	203 ,,	
Swellendam ...	Cape Town	126 ,,	
Tulbagh ...	Cape Town	76 ,,	Rail, Western System.
Uitenhage ...	Algoa Bay	21 ,,	Rail, Midland System.
Utrecht ...	Durban ...	210 ,,	
Victoria, West	Algoa Bay	425 ,,	420 miles by Rail, Midland and Western
,,	Cape Town	426 ,,	419 miles by Rail, Western System.
Weenen ...	Cape Town	130 ,,	
Wellington ...	Cape Town	45 ,,	Rail, Western System.
Worcester ...	Durban ...	109 ,,	Rail, Western System.
Wynberg ...	Cape Town	8 ,,	Rail, Western System.

The Union Steam Ship Company, Limited.

THE SOUTH AFRICAN GOLD FIELDS.

The Chief Centres of the Gold Fields in the Transvaal are JOHANNESBURG (Witwatersrandt) and BARBERTON, which can be reached either from Cape Town, Port Elizabeth (Algoa Bay), East London, Durban (Natal), or Delagoa Bay.

The following information with reference to the means of communication between these Ports and the Gold Fields is given without responsibility and is subject to alteration :—

To JOHANNESBURG (Witwatersrandt).

	Miles	Hours	Fares.
From CAPE TOWN to Kimberley by Rail ...	647	32	
Kimberley to Johannesburg by Coach ...	298	53	
	945	85	
From PORT ELIZABETH to Kimberley by Rail	485	27	
Kimberley to Johannesburg by Coach ...	285	57	
	770	84	
From EAST LONDON to Aliwal North by rail	280	24	
Aliwal North to Johannesburg by Coach	330	144	
	610	168	
From DURBAN (Natal) to Ladysmith by Rail	189	15	
Ladysmith to Johannesburg by Coach ...	200	57	(Including stoppages, 27 hours actual travelling)
	389	72	
From DELAGOA BAY to Komati by rail ...	55	3	
Komati to Johannesburg, about	300	112	
	355	115	

To BARBERTON.

	Miles	Hours
From CAPE TOWN to Kimberley by Rail ...	647	32
Kimberley to Barberton by Coach ...	530	132
	1,177	164
From PORT ELIZABETH to Kimberley by Rail	485	27
Kimberley to Barberton by Coach ...	530	132
	1,015	159
From DURBAN (Natal) to Ladysmith by Rail	189	15
Ladysmith to Barberton	285	104
	474	119

Mule Waggons also leave Ladysmith, taking Passengers at a lower fare than by Coach.

From DELAGOA BAY to Komati by rail ...	55	3
Komati to Barberton, about	60	72
	115	75

UNION STEAM SHIP COMPANY, LIMITED.
(ESTABLISHED 1853.)

DIRECTORS.

ALFRED GILES, Esq., M.P., CHAIRMAN.

F. H. EVANS, Esq., M.P., DEPUTY-CHAIRMAN.

W. M. FARMER, Esq.
H. W. MAYNARD, Esq.
LT.-GEN. F. MARSHALL.
W. S. NICHOLSON, Esq.
W. J. ROHMER, Esq.

Secretary—E. AUBREY HART, Esq.

OFFICES AND AGENCIES

UNITED KINGDOM.

OFFICES:

LONDON, 11, LEADENHALL STREET.
　　West End Agency: G. W. WHEATLEY & Co., 23, Regent Street, S.W.
SOUTHAMPTON, ORIENTAL PLACE.

Superintendent Agents for —

CORNWALL & DEVON, H. J. WARING & Co., The Wharf, Millbay, Plymouth.

AGENTS:

ABERDEEN, J. S. CHALMERS, 56, Marischal Street.
BELFAST, A. A. WATT, 3, Custom House Square.
BIRMINGHAM, {J. F. BRAME, Union Chambers, Union Passage
　　　　　　　{W. H. HAYWARD, 42, Union Passage.
BRADFORD (YORK), W. H. RILEY, 2, Currer Street.
BRISTOL, HENRY R. JAMES, 8, Queen's Square.
CORK, WELLS & HOLOHAN, 3, Penrose Quay.
DUBLIN, CAROLIN & EGAN, 30, Eden Quay.
　　　　　 {J. A. ANDERSON, 6, St. Andrew Street.
DUNDEE. {HENDERSON BROS., 1, Panmure Street.
　　　　　 {J. & A. ALLAN, 4, India Buildings.

The Union Steam Ship Company, Limited.

UNITED KINGDOM—*(continued)*.

EDINBURGH, A. O. OTTYWELL, 6, Shandwick Place.
GLASGOW, F. W. ALLAN & Co., 125, Buchanan Street.
HULL, H. J. BARRETT, 17, High Street.
LEEDS, W. H. PINDER, 166, Woodhouse Lane.
LIVERPOOL, F. STUMORE & Co., 20, Water Street.
LONDONDERRY, F. DAWSON, 42, Foyle Street.
MANCHESTER, KELLER, WALLIS & Co., 69, Piccadilly.
NEWCASTLE-ON-TYNE, JAMES POTTS & SON, 26, Sandhill.
NOTTINGHAM, SANDERSON & Co., 12, Heathcote Street, and 30, Wheeler Gate.
PORTSMOUTH { J. BLAKE & SON, 170, Queen Street, Portsea.
{ CURTISS & SONS, Railway and Shipping Agents.
SHEFFIELD, T. CLARKE, 52, Harvest Lane.
WATERFORD, T. S. HARVEY & SON, 12, Little Georges Street.
YORK, W. PICKWELL, 1, High Jubbergate.
(AND IN MOST PROVINCIAL TOWNS.)
MESSRS. THOS. COOK & SON, LUDGATE CIRCUS, LONDON, E.C., and at all Branches.
MESSRS. GAZE & SON, 142, STRAND, LONDON, W.C., and at all Branches.
MESSRS. NIXON & KING, 40, PICCADILLY CIRCUS, LONDON, W.
INTERNATIONAL SLEEPING CAR COMPANY, 123, PALL MALL, LONDON, S.W.

COLONIAL.

MADEIRA	BLANDY BROS. & Co.
ST. HELENA	SOLOMON, MOSS, GIDEON & Co.
SIMON'S TOWN	W. ANDERSON & Co.
CAPE TOWN (CAPE OF GOOD HOPE)	T. E. FULLER, Esq., M.L.A., Chief Agent for South Africa, Union Steam Ship Co. E. W. STEELE, Esq., Agent.
MOSSEL BAY	J. MUDIE.
KNYSNA	G. W. B. STEYTLER.
ALGOA BAY	A. WATSON, Esq., Union Steam Ship Co.
PORT ALFRED (KOWIE RIVER), CAPE OF GOOD HOPE	J. BLACK & Co. (Mr. C. A. Bezant)
GRAHAM'S TOWN (CAPE OF GOOD HOPE)	,, ,,
EAST LONDON	DYER & DYER.
KING WILLIAM'S TOWN	,, ,,
PAARL	J. J. DE VILLIERS.
UNIONDALE	TAYLDER & BOOTH.
MURRAYSBURG	J. H. DALY.
WORCESTER	BERNARD & Co.
SWELLENDAM	J. GREATHEAD & Co.
QUEEN'S TOWN	J. HODGES & Co.

COLONIAL—(continued).

GRAAFF REINET (Cape of Good Hope) A. Goldman.
GEORGE TOWN ,, ,, George Row.
BEAUFORT WEST ,, ,, Honel. C. Pritchard.
CRADOCK ,, ,, J. W. Stevens & Co.
RICHMOND ,, ,, R. Mortimer & Co.
COLESBERG ,, ,, Wills & Fryer.
FORT BEAUFORT ,, ,, Savage & Hill.
OUDTSHORN ,, ,, Taute & Co.
BURGHERSDORP ,, ,, John Blake.
BEDFORD .. .. C. Thorne.
SOMERSET EAST .. .. .. De Wet & Leisching.
DURBAN, Natal (South Africa) H.J.Watts, Esq., UnionSteamShipCo.
PIETERMARITZBURG, Natal Do. .. C. E. Taunton.
KOKSTAD .. .. H. & T. McCubbin.
HARRISMITH .. .. McKechnie Bros.
LADYSMITH .. ..
NEWCASTLE .. .. R. D. Kidd & Co.
KIMBERLEY, Diamond Fields.. .. Woollan Bros.
BLOEMFONTEIN (Orange Free State)Barlow Bros. & Co.
FAURESMITH Do. C. Dowsett.
POTCHEFSTROOM (Transvaal, South Africa), Reid & Co.
KLERKSDORP .. .. Higson & Trevor-Smith.
LYDENBURG (Transvaal, South Africa) } J. H. Parker.
PILGRIM'S REST ,, ,,
HEIDELBERG ,, ,, E. W. Noyce.
KLERKSDORP .. ..
BARBERTON (Transvaal Gold Fields) Diamond & Co.
JOHANNESBURG (Witwatersrandt) C. Cowen & Co.
PRETORIA (Transvaal, South Africa) D. M. Kisch.
DELAGOA BAY (East Africa) .. The Oost-Afrikaansche Co.
INHAMBANE ,, ,, .. ,, ,,
QUILLIMANE ,, ,, .. Senor Nunes.
MOZAMBIQUE ,, ,, .. Fabre & Son.
MAURITIUS .. .. Blyth Bros. & Co., Port Louis.
TAMATAVE (Madagascar) .. .. Porter, Aitken & Co.

CONTINENTAL, &c.

AMSTERDAM, De Vries & Co.
ANCONA. L. Claasen & Co.
ANTWERP, John P. Best & Co., and at Ghent, Flushing and Terneuzen.
ARNHEM, Junius & Co.
BASLE. Schneebeli & Co.
BERGEN, N. Lovold.
BERLIN, Brasch and Rothenstein.

BILBAO, F. De Gana & Clark.
BORDEAUX, V. Depas, 4, Rue Lafayette.
BOULOGNE, A. Henry & Co.
BREMEN, J. H. Bachmann.
BREST, Kerros & Fils.
CADIZ, Daniel McPherson.
CALAIS, A. Langlet & Co.

The Union Steam Ship Company, Limited. 215

CONTINENTAL, &c.—(continued).

CANNES, The Banque du Commerce
CATANIA, G. Galatioto.
CHRISTIANIA, F. Lie.
CHRISTIANSAND, T. C. Hansen.
COLOGNE, W. Pagenstecher.
COPENHAGEN, R. H. Reeh.
CORUNNA, Nicholas M. Del Rio.
DRESDEN, Ernst Strack.
DUNKIRK, Léon Herbart.
DORTMUND } Brasch and
EISENACH } Rothenstein.
FLORENCE, T. Romieux.
FRANKFORT O/M { J. Schottenfels & Co. C. H. Textor.
GENOA & SAVONA, Gondrand Freres.
GIBRALTAR, Thos. Mosley & Co.
GOTHENBURG, J. Odell.
GRONINGEN, Prinz & Zwanenberg.
HAMBURG, John Suhr.
HARLINGEN, T. G. Van Slooten.
HAVRE, Langstaff, Ehrenberg and Pollak.
LA ROCHELLE, Michel & Fils.
LEGHORN, Wm. Miller, Robley & Co.
LEIPZIG, Brasch & Rothenstein.
LISBON, Knowles, Rawes & Co.
LYONS, J. Chirat & Cie.
MADRID, E. Bourcoud.
MALTA, O. F. Gollcher & Sons.
MANNHEIM, Conrad Herold.
MARSEILLES, A. Fabre & Fils.

MESSINA, Fratelli Greco.
MATHA & SAINTES (France), G. Guiberteau.
MILAN, J. Mangili.
NAPLES, Holme & Co.
NEW YORK { Henderson Bros., 7, Bowling Green. Barber & Co., 35, Broadway.
OSTEND, A. & J. Van Iseghem.
OPORTO, A. J. Shore & Co.
PALERMO, Conrad A. Kandler.
PARIS, G. Dunlop & Co., 38, Avenue de l'Opera, and 26, Rue d'Hauteville.
ROTTERDAM, Kuyper, Van Dam and Smeer.
ST. MALO, J. C. Amy.
ST. GALL, (Switzerland), Niebergall & Goth.
STAVANGER, A. L. Svensden.
STUTTGART { Schmidt & Dihlmann. Brasch & Rothenstein.
TENERIFFE, Hamilton & Co.
TEXEL, Koning & Co.
TONNAY-CHARENTE, Renault Delage and Co.
TRIESTE, Giuseppe Basevi.
VENICE { S. & A. Blumenthal. Fratelli Pardo di Giuseppe.
VIGO, M. Barçena-y-Franco

W. B. WHITTINGHAM & CO., Printers, 91, Gracechurch Street, London.

www.ingramcontent.com/pod-product-compliance
Lightning Source LLC
Chambersburg PA
CBHW032108220426
43664CB00008B/1173